JOSEPH COVINO JR

UWF:
UNIVERSITY
OF
WEST
("WORST")
FLORIDA
EXPOSED!

EPIC PRESS

Published by:
Epic Press
PO Box 30108
Walnut Creek, CA 94598

First *Epic Press* Edition published 2008

FOR

DR ERSKINE S DOTTIN,

KNIGHT ERRANT

OF

ACADEMIC

AND

INTELLECTUAL

FREEDOM,

FREE SPEECH

AND

FREE EXPRESSION

CONTENTS

PART I:

PROLOGUE

(CORRUPT BASTARDS)

ONE:
BACKSTORY

"We are pleased to note that you(Mr. Joseph Covino, Jr.)have been awarded the **Alexander Wilbourne Weddell Award** *for 1974–75. We should like to present you at the Commencement of Columbian College of Arts and Sciences... Congratulations on this honor."—***Robert G. Jones, University Marshal, GWU, 25 April 1975**

§

"I am very pleased to tell you(Mr. Joseph Covino)that you have been awarded the ***Alexander Wilbourne Weddell Prize***. *This Prize is awarded annually to the candidate for a degree who writes the best essay on the subject of 'the promotion of peace among the nations of the world.' I congratulate you most heartily on your achievement and extend every good wish for a successful future."—***Calvin D. Linton, Dean, Columbian College of Arts and Sciences, GWU, 1 May 1975**

I t all began with the remarkably regressive academic relapse I was forced to suffer out of sheer monetary privation.

At just 17 I left an extremely dysfunctional, conflict–plagued family home to start my senior year at Florida's Roman Catholic diocesan *Pensacola Catholic High School(CHS)*where I excelled in such extracurricular activities as band, forensics(public speaking)and track, graduating in May 1972 as a *National Honor Society(NHS)*student.

Following high school I attended *Pensacola Junior College(PJC)*where I participated for an academic year in student government, acting as the community college's student public defender and graduating with a general associate in arts(AA)degree in August 1974.

For a single winter semester in 1975 I attended the top–tier *School of Government and Business Administration(SGBA)*at the private co–educational *George Washington University(GWU)*in Washington, DC, where I won the *Alexander Wilbourne Weddell Prize*—established in 1923 by Virginia Chase Weddell in memory of her husband and awarded annually to a degree candidate writing the best essay on "the promotion of peace among the nations of the world."

That essay writing award was conferred by *GWU*'s *Columbian College of Arts and Sciences(CCAS)*and I was the sole junior–level student so honored at the university's spring graduation commencement exercises in May 1975.

Throughout this entire scholastic time I was virtually a penniless student. From just 19 onward I'd been living alone, completely on my own and completely self–supporting—without anyone's charity—working at such odd jobs as supermarket clerk, auto parts deliveryman, college dormitory night watchman, brass musical instrument repairman, taxicab driver, airport shuttle chauffeur and credit bureau clerk. Neither family nor friends(I had no family and few friends)lent me the least financial assistance towards paying for my so–called "higher education." Until I was 22–23 my income was luckily supplemented respectively by paltry monthly social security and veteran's survivors benefits paid on behalf of my father, a US Army veteran, who'd died in 1972.

Whatever I'd accomplished educationally by then, despite being economically disadvantaged, I'd done mostly by myself—by my own devices. I was no idle loafer or layabout student born with a silver spoon in my mouth. I was merely a hardworking kid making his own way in a coldly indifferent and unconcerned world—a poor kid who couldn't afford to go to a rich kid's school.

Being compelled by sheer economic necessity to leave the top–flight but extremely costly *George Washington University(GWU)*to enroll at Pensacola's far inferior(but much cheaper)public co–educational *University of West("Worst")Florida(UWF)*was for me then a supremely sad and bitter disappointment!

Winding up in my backwater hick town of Pensacola to attend UWF was not only a humongous letdown but I hadn't a clue about what to possibly study there that might be the least bit interesting, challenging, useful or beneficial in life—whether academically, professionally or vocationally. Well, it came to my knowledge that our country's current president–by–default, **Gerald Rudolph Ford, Jr**, had graduated from the *University of Michigan* in 1935 with a degree in economics and political science. So on one of my worst and most impulsive whims I decided to major likewise in economics at UWF—a major blunder-

12

ing mistake but a flash point in my destiny besides.

This then is the sometimes sordid story of how several pompous and imperious bureaucratic functionaries, comprising the corrupt good old boy network at the *University of West(Worst)Florida(UWF)*—from the combined offices of financial aid director, collections manager, controller, business manager, academic affairs vice president, student affairs vice president, university registrar, housing director to even the university president himself—conspired in concert together to gang up administratively and wage bureaucratic warfare on one lone strapped student—in their impotent attempts to stifle and suppress his First Amendment rights of free speech and expression. It's the successful story of how that solitary student joined issue and defied, opposed, resisted and eventually thwarted all their conniving and scheming plots against him, making *monkeys* of them all—which admittedly in most cases wasn't too much of a stretch! The sole arms he ever took up against the fools throughout this freedom struggle were his own creative imagination, ideas and words! Ultimately it's the triumphant story of the *POWER OF THE PEN* over the petty and spiteful schemes and designs of ruthlessly malicious and evil–minded men!

TWO:

CRAPPY "COUNSELING"

*"I wish to congratulate you(Mr Joseph Covino Jr)for achieving the Provost's Honor Roll in Alpha College for Spring Quarter, 1976. Your grade point average of **3.83** for your recent course work reflects ability as well as motivation and initiative...we are particularly gratified about your academic performance."*—**Lucius F Ellsworth, Provost, Alpha College, UWF, 22 June 1976.**

"IDON'T GET PAID A DAMN DIME TO LISTEN TO YOU!"** local moneybags *Mutual Federal Savings and Loan Association* chairman and *Florida Regent, EW Hopkins*, rudely responded to my attempt to explain to him my academic predicament by telephone.

*"I have discussed issues raised by you in our conversation...vis–a–vis graduation requirements for your bachelor's degree in Economics with **Provost(Lucius F)Ellsworth**. He assures me that the **Money and Banking** course is deemed essential to your program by your advisor,"* UWF academic affairs vice president, **Arthur H Doerr**, wrote me in his condescending letter dated 19 July 1976. *"I realize, of course, that different individuals view the counseling process in different ways, but faculty members assure me that **Money and Banking** is important in your background."*

Pompous academicians really get off on resorting to misused expressions(like *"vis–a–vis"*)in their lame–ass, piss–poor attempts to come off sounding profound.

That bloated Provost Ellsworth(Dunce Doerr mentions)was a perfectly polished and supreme *bastard!*

In the very same apologetic breath schmuck Ellsworth pointed out that the university academic catalog was "not a contract" but that the nebulous "counselor" could indeed arbitrarily add graduation requirements to the economics degree program. That nebulous "counselor," he'd posit, arbitrarily designed the student's degree program—not necessarily in consultation with the student so put upon.

"On July 15," Schmuck Ellsworth wrote in his memo dated that very same 19 July 1976 to knave

economics professor, **Frank E. Ranelli**, found in my economics department file and obtained under the federal **Family Educational Rights and Privacy Act(the FERPA or Buckley Amendment, 1974)**, *"I reviewed Mr. Covino's appeal for a waiver of the requirement that he take a course in Money and Banking before he graduates. It was determined that his advisor, **Professor Janet Miller**, had informed him of the requirement **several quarters** ago and that he had avoided taking the course; that his chairman has supported the advisor's decision; ...*

*"I have informed Mr. Covino that I rejected his appeal because he was **aware** of the requirement and that the requirement was **reasonable** for an economics major..."*

Like most of his bureaucratic cohorts in UWF's corrupt good old boy network, Schmuck Ellsworth was and is an out and out *LIAR!*

That nebulous "advisor" had sprung that so–called *un*–reasonable "requirement" on me at the very last minute at the onset of my graduation quarter via some memo which even the economics department secretary didn't notice until I went to sign my so–called "degree planning sheet."

Conveniently that nebulous "advisor" Dunce Doerr refers to remains nameless as those nebulous "faculty members" remain faceless.

Those "issues" taken by me *in opposition to*(not *"vis–a–vis"*)certain supposed UWF "graduation requirements" comprised the first major bone of contention between me and this minor(abysmal)institution of lower learning—which Dunce Doerr, acting as academic apologist, attempted so lamely to gloss over and explain away: this stupid twerp of an "academic advisor," so–called, was trying just as lamely to force me to take their worthless finance department course(*"money and banking"*)as an official requisite condition for me to graduate from worthless UWF with its equally worthless bachelor's degree in economics!

The only trouble was: that particular finance department course—*"money and banking"*—was a legitimate "graduation requirement," so–called, for neither the economics department in particular nor the university at large!

So the patently phony claim that this useless *elective "money and banking"* course ever constituted a valid "graduation requirement" was a moot point from the start.

Naturally I went through the token motions of officially appealing that inexplicably compulsory "graduation requirement" to the university's highest head honchos.

"I am sure you realize that Faculties recommend students to receive degrees, and Faculties determine the requirements for those degrees," wrote penguin–looking UWF president, **James A Robinson**, in his excruciatingly condescending letter dated 27 July 1976. *"You have assumed a superficial consideration of your petition by those to whom you have appealed. The investigation, which was not superficial, yielded information which caused both the Provost and Vice President to take a different decision from one which you would have taken...I do regret that you feel you have been badly treated, but I do not agree that you have received cavalier treatment from responsible administrative officials."*

Arbitrary, capricious and corrupt—not "cavalier"—is, quite the contrary, how I'd characterize UWF's imperious and irresponsible "administrative officials" in this case! And their supposed "consideration of(my) petition" not "superficial," but rather *inconsequential!*

In his letter dated 25 October 1976, Florida Governor Reubin O'D Askew's proxy "Education Coordinator," **Marshall A Harris**, concurred that my *"protest lacked merit on both substantive and procedural questions."*

To reiterate: UWF's economics department "faculty" never "determined" the *elective* finance department course—*"money and banking"*—to be a graduation requirement for an economics bachelor's degree! It was a "requirement" fully fabricated on the wholly arbitrary and capricious whim of one quirky "counselor."

Admittedly I was anxious and eager to graduate with *any* academic degree being the first in my dysfunctional family ever to do so. What I objected to most though was getting forcibly crammed down my throat by this uppity lowlife biddy named "Mrs."(*not* "Dr.")**Janet S Miller**, a mightily arrogant economics instructor posing as an academic advisor in that department, that so–called *"money and banking"* course for which I'd be compelled against my better judgment to waste time, effort and money(I didn't have)passing!

Not knowing me from Adam that uppity biddy called my dire financial straits a "sob story"—that I was virtually a destitute student without a car who actually had to hitchhike some *ten miles* across town on a daily basis just to get to the university since no city bus went directly to campus.

"You made a farce of the entire counseling process," she chastised me for consulting in the matter another admirable advisor, associate economics professor **Dr. James H Dukes**, whom she claimed gave me "bad advice," confirming that the course in contention was no bachelor's degree requirement according to the university's academic catalog, which took rightful precedence over any counselor's arbitrary and capricious quirks.

"You gambled and lost," she presumed to reprimand me concerning my free choice to change counselors during my last graduation quarter—my just and legitimate prerogative. I sure as hell never asked to have *her* assigned as my academic advisor in the first place!

Somebody "could" simply waive the supposed course graduation requirement, she admitted, and she herself could've "negotiated" the supposed requirement "before but not after the fact."

"I won't waive it now," the uppity biddy boasted adamantly but privately that Friday the 27th of August 1976, "because you backed me up against the wall by your appeals."

If I made a mockery of the counseling "process" it was **Janet S Miller** who made a mockery of the counseling function by perverting it to a malicious, retaliatory act of personality politics—not caring a tinker's damn about the adverse consequences provoked by her petty spite.

The pure and simple truth of the matter was that any supposed counseling "process" was totally nonexistent from the git–go:

There'd never been any counseling consultations. The very first time that I ever found out about Miller's arbitrary and capricious course requirement was when I visited the economics department(to sign my so–called degree graduation "planning sheet" which Miller claimed was a binding "contract")where some *student assistant* in the department secretary's office read to me a supposed "memo" from Miller—a small scrap of scratch paper indicating the required *"money and banking"* course. Out and out outrageous!

On a subsequent visit to that office the department *secretary* herself confirmed that I'd already completed that "planning sheet" and couldn't comprehend herself *why* Miller was so adamantly trying to compel me to take a wholly irrelevant course *not* formally required by the university academic catalog for the bachelor's degree in economics. During those office visits Miller herself was always and ever nowhere to be found!

Why then was no esoteric mystery to me: the hyper–frustrated biddy was super–high on some feminist–fanatic power–trip!

Even knave associate economics professor, **Dr. FE Ranelli**, tried to weasel his way into the act at the last minute, colluding with Miller to require me to take for graduation a statistics course, which unbeknownst to them I'd already completed at the local community college.

Only time would tell though who'd be the real *LOSER* in the end!

Unbeknownst to clueless Miller I'd already hatched an alternative plot: the very day before the 26th of August 1976 my *change of academic major* from the *economics* to the **criminal justice** department had been officially approved! In December 1976 I graduated from worthless UWF with my first worthless bachelor's degree in **criminal justice!**

I outright refused and never took the **money and banking** course Miller tried so ineffectually cramming down my throat!

*"He has **sacrificed** a great deal in order to complete his undergraduate studies,"* wrote **Joseph R. Youd,**

Jr., Vice President & Cashier, *Bank of Pensacola*, in his recommendation letter for me dated 9 February 1977. *"I have never met an individual who would have gone through what Joe has gone through over the past four years...He is a man of high character and morals and will always stand up for high beliefs even when it brings him **hardships**."*

THREE:

LEAKY SYSTEMS

"I am pleased to inform you(Mr Joseph Covino)that as a result of your excellent academic performance you are being named to the Provost's Honor Roll for the Fall Quarter, 1976. I know that this academic record comes about only as a result of hard work and a commitment to high performance on your part, and I commend you for your efforts. The faculty of the college is truly proud to formally honor students of your caliber."—H. T. Martin, Jr., Provost, Omega College, UWF, 10 January 1977

"Ican understand your perplexity, though your rage suggests to me that you have not yet discovered the universality of the axiom, 'All systems *leak*,'" wrote **Richard B. Hauch**, Acting apologist Chairman, UWF's Faculty of English and Foreign Languages, in his condescending, white-washing letter to me dated 15 November 1976.

Hauch was responding to my letter dated 4 November 1976 expressing conspicuous displeasure—not "rage"—with the incredibly inept manner in which his department had administered to me its namby–pamby "EH 301 writing proficiency test" on the last day of final exams the previous *summer* quarter, neglecting yet to report to me whether I'd passed or failed the test by the end of the following *fall* quarter.

Actually I'd failed that three–part test because the department *secretary* proctoring it called time on me and collected it before I could even finish its third and final section; I was taking that stupid test to pad a 2.5–hour credit "deficiency" in my academic program.

My perfectly legitimate beef was that no one on their not–so–eminent "examining committee" had yet notified me that I'd failed or why—because, it came out, they'd had most presumptuously assumed that I'd voluntarily elected in mid–test not to complete it! Utterly unbelievable!

"Dr.(A. Michael)Yots," Hauck wrote me in his pre-ceding excuse–making letter dated 29 October 1976, *"reports that you were not informed you had failed the examination because it appears...that you decided to give up the examination attempt...Naturally, this much evidence of your writing ability cannot by any stretch of the imagination constitute a passing per-*

formance for credit. I also believe that it was quite **logical** *for the examining committee to conclude that you had indeed decided to change your mind about continuing the attempt to get credit by examination for EH 301."*

Pretty warped **logic** based principally upon mindless punch–drunk presumption!

"As a matter of fact," Hauck admitted in his subsequent letter, *"you did complete the other sections of the test, but that is not the point: you did not complete the section of the test which bears the burden of revealing whether or not you can write."*

There I was an honors student and award–winning writer on the verge of graduating with my first of *three* equally worthless UWF bachelor's degrees and this bureaucratic clod's wondering whether I can write! Utterly unbelievable!

"I have informed the professors concerned that, regardless of their impressions," Hauck concluded in that subsequent letter, *"they should have informed you in a timely fashion that you had failed the test."*

Right on, brother! All lame–ass, piss–poor excuses aside that's all I was ever griping about! But die–hard apologists invariably make endless excuses to gloss over and explain away their own blundering to the very bitter end!

"In going through materials from the five months(August–December)I was on leave," **Stanton Millet**, Chairman, Faculty of English and Foreign Languages, Alpha College, UWF, ultimately vindicated me in his apologetic letter dated 11 January 1977, *"I have just come across your exchange of correspondence regarding your EH 301 proficiency examination results...*

"I am sorry these scores were not reported to you

when you first inquired."

Well, better late than never!

About UWF I'd already formed my own "axiom": all "systems" don't merely "leak"—they freakin' *FLOOD!*

And by no "stretch of the imagination" could any amount of alibis or denial ever conceivably smooth over the situation of: UWF's *rampant* incompetence and ineptitude!

FOUR:

ECONOMICS

SUCCESS

*"Dr. Ellsworth has passed on to me the materials you sent him concerning your desire to complete a Baccalaureate degree in Economics. I agree that you(Mr. Joseph Covino, Jr.)have satisfied all the requirements for the degree and have notified the Registrar to add you to the Summer Quarter, 1979 graduation list."—**R.C. Einbecker, Dean, College of Business, UWF, 9 August 1979***

From roughly March 1977 through August 1978 I'd taken a self–imposed but most welcome sabbatical from both my backwater hometown of Pensacola and the *University of "Worst" Florida(UWF)*when I accompanied my *Phi Theta Kappa(PTK)*honor society student girlfriend, Jean, to Boca Raton, Florida to attend the public, upper–level, co–educational, *Florida Atlantic University(FAU)*, where I enrolled in post–graduate studies in both political science and secondary education.

During my last summer quarter at that commuter school the sterling opportunity, which I took timely advantage of, presented itself for me to take within its College of Social Science the economics course *4223 Money—paid for* most significantly *not* by me but rather by *non*–repayable financial aid graduate *grant* funds—which turned out to satisfy the arbitrary and capricious finance department *"money and banking"* course(*FIN 3233*)requirement for my economics bachelor's degree, which in turn imperious UWF officials had set for me to meet.

First I quietly made some discreet inquiries of UWF to determine whether the two courses were actually equivalent and received in return some initial but irrational resistance.

*"I have received information from Mr. **Hal Harden** in Admissions concerning your question as to whether ECO 4223 equals our FIN 3233, **Money and Banking** course. Mr. Harden informs me that the two courses are **not** equal. Therefore, you **cannot** substitute one for the other,"* wrote **C.C. Elebash**, Chairman, Alpha College, UWF, in his letter to me dated 18 September 1978.

*"I hope this does not present too big a **problem** for*

you," Elebash added pompously.

Functionary Elebash was a flunky of Provost **Lucius F Ellsworth** but his lame–ass, piss–poor attempt to thwart the transfer of that economics "money" course from FAU to UWF was way too little, too late, as I'd already secured independent confirmation of the equivalence of the two courses from the college's former chairman before he absconded from UWF.

"At any rate," wrote **James H. Potts**, Chairman, Alpha College, UWF, in his previous letter to me dated 8 June 1978, *"the answer to your question is **yes**, the courses are **equivalent**. If you need any further information, please let me know."*

Further information was then indeed needed since Chairman Potts hadn't *specified* the equivalent course *numbers* in his confirmation letter.

By September 1978 though Chairman Potts had taken flight from *UWF* to Johnson City, Tennessee to *East Tennessee State University* where he assumed that school's accounting department chairmanship.

"Whatever I told you on 6/8/78 I stick by," Chairman Potts confirmed more specifically in his hand–written note to me postmarked 29 June 1979. *"The courses are **'equivalent'** therefore ECO 4223 should substitute for FIN 3233. I see no **problem**. But, I am not chairman at UWF. I have **no** authority there. Best of luck. Jim Potts."*

No *"problem"* indeed since I'd taken the additional precaution of securing independent confirmation of the course equivalents from other bureaucratic quarters at UWF.

"In response to your request," wrote **Patricia J. Whitfield**, Director, Records and Registration, UWF, wrote me in her letter dated 26 June 1979, *"the Department of Finance and Accounting has*

determined that the course ECO 4223 at Florida Atlantic University will substitute for FIN 3233 at this University."

Craftily I'd even written the professors teaching both the equivalent economics and finance department **"money and banking"** courses at both FAU and UWF respectively to secure confirmation of even the **textbooks** used in teaching those courses. A long–shot bright idea perhaps but, unfortunately, those *textbooks* did *not* match up!

"If you are to be an accounting and finance student at the University of West Florida," equivocated **Gregory C. Yost**, Interim Chairman, Alpha College, UWF, in his letter to me dated 28 June 1979, *"we will accept Florida Atlantic's ECO 4223 in lieu of our FIN 3233. However, I cannot speak for **other departments**."*

"Other departments," referring quite obliquely of course to UWF's **economics** department—still at the heart of that entire bone of contention.

Die–hard bureaucratic functionaries rarely give up once they've set out for whatever warped motivation to frustrate the academic aspirations of students they're supposed to service. Nor did I give up either.

By August 1979 UWF's business college dean, **R. C. Einbecker**, had come through for me once more by approving as fulfilled all my academic graduation requirements for yet a second worthless bachelor's degree in **economics** from worthless UWF!

Nearly *three* years earlier as Assistant Provost, Omega College, UWF(from which I'd already graduated with that first worthless bachelor's degree in **criminal justice**)**Richard C. Einbecker** went the extra proverbial mile in my absence of personally reviewing all my course work, confirming for me in writing the 20th of December *1976* that I'd met all graduation requirements and releasing me from the silly chore of personally signing my so–called "Degree Planning Sheet" on account of the great difficulty it took a poor pedestrian such as myself to commute to that damned, god–forsaken campus so remotely located *ten* miles outside of town—not served then even by mass transit!

"I want to take this opportunity to congratulate you on completing your baccalaureate degree and please let me know if I can help you in any way in the future," Assistant Provost Einbecker wrote me kindly in closing.

"Mr. Covino," Einbecker wrote **Pat Whitfield** in his memo dated 9 August 1979 found in my economics department file obtained under the federal **Family Educational Rights and Privacy Act(the FERPA or Buckley Amendment, 1974)**, *"has completed all the requirements for a Baccalaureate degree in Economics, and I would appreciate it if you would add him to the graduation list for Summer Quarter, 1979."*

At UWF the old adage that only bastards and cream rise to the top proved invariably true but **Richard Charles Einbecker** was an exceptional exception to that rule. And when the time came for me *three* years later to submit my "materials"(as he termed them)for graduation from worthless UWF with a second worthless bachelor's degree in **economics**, UWF business college dean **RC Einbecker** was most instrumentally—and invaluably—placed!

§

Curiously contained in my official UWF student

economics department file—obtained under the federal ***Family Educational Rights and Privacy Act(FERPA, the Buckley Amendment, 1974)***—I found a copy of this ***letter–to–the–editor*** I'd written to the local *Escambia County **BEACON*** community newspaper dated ***23 September 1976***—my name circled and the piece headed with the underscored, scrawled name: ***Lucius!*** Reproduced in its entirety:

*"Certain University of West Florida members must be brought accountable. I'm an honor's list student declining to waste money on an elective course(Money and Banking)recommended by economics counselor **Janet Miller**—claiming I never made my double–degree objective "very clear" though two different graduation forms filed at both departments specify otherwise.*

*"Two academic quarters before scheduled graduation, a student assistant presided over the signing of my degree planning sheet, reading me a small memo–suggestion from an absentee Miller that I take Money and Banking, a course **NOT** an official UWF catalog requirement and **NOT** required for completion by all economics majors. I wasn't issued a copy of the planning sheet—provisions of which can be easily added to or subtracted from.*

"Too, a second economics counselor informed me the UWF catalog took precedence over any counselor's prerogative—otherwise electives could be added to my requirements indefinitely.

"A week into my graduation quarter(Miller was in Europe), Economics Chairman Ranelli approved adding a social welfare course to my schedule, having the opportunity to add Money and Banking after reviewing my file containing Miller's absentee memo.

"I've completed the 35 economics hours and the 90

hours needed for any bachelor's degree. I can't gradu-ate. Administrators won't waive the elective. Board of Regents Hopkins said, **"I don't get paid a damn dime to listen to you."**

"Ramifications: adding to my $3400 educational debt; forcing me to bus and hitch–hike to UWF from downtown(I have no car and transit service ends at West Florida Hospital); depriving me of job hours.

"Calling me a 'sob story,' Miller refused to waive the course because I went to another counselor for what she termed 'bad advice.' Miller accused me of 'making a farce' of the counseling process—farcical long before I ever arrived.

"I've earned and paid for university service, not hindrance. What justification exists for knowingly putting four hard–worked years of education on the line for no good reason?"

§

Schmuck Ellsworth was already keeping very close and careful tabs on me even then. Be *afraid*, Schmuck Ellsworth, be *VERY afraid!*

FIVE:

CORDIAL

CREEP,

CR BENNETT

"**Y**our application for a Federally Insured Student Loan," UWF financial aid director, **C.R. Bennett**, wrote me in his condescending letter dated 3 August 1979, *"beginning Fall Quarter, 1979, has been processed by this office. It is procedure to discuss in person the application before release when certain questions raised by information on the application and/or issues tangential to the application remain unresolved.* **Until** *you comply with my phone request of August 1, 1979, via* **Nell Peazant**, *Financial Aid Counselor, for a personal appointment, the* **Federally Insured Student Loan** *application will* **not** *be released to you."*

That **Nell Peazant** was one remarkably rude biddy who habitually exercised to the hilt her civil right of incivility!

Take special note though of Blockhead Bennett's last conditional *until–you–do–this–we–won't–do–that* line of the letter.

Bullying bureaucratic coercion was a practiced specialty of UWF officials at large and in particular of **CR Bennett**, who got off on abusing and misusing his position as financial aid director to dictatorially *deny* rather than grant—through his personally prejudiced and judgmental "screening" practices—the *most* financial aid applicants possible!

"In response to your recent request," Blockhead Bennett followed up with his next deliberately stonewalling letter dated 8 August 1979, *"it will not be necessary for you to complete the application process as it has been brought to my attention that you are now pursuing a* **second Bachelor's** *degree. Because of a limited allocation of funds it has become necessary for this office to discontinue disbursements of col-*

lege–based aid to students working on their **second Bachelor's** *and/or Master's degree. If you should decide to pursue the application process and/or for your own records, your file is lacking Financial Aid Transcripts for Pensacola Junior College and George Washington University."*

"Cordially," was the recurring closure with which Blockhead Bennett habitually signed all of his painfully pompous letters.

His dopey informant's intelligence was as inexact as it was out–of–date. UWF had already approved my change–of–major from **criminal justice** to **international studies**—for pursuit of a **third** worthless UWF **bachelor's** degree—*months* before since 6 *April* 1979. Blockhead Bennett—in his fanatical and malicious zeal to prevent me from attending UWF at all—was an **IDIOT** to boot! In all his evil–minded, ill–intended designs against me though he'd fail miserably.

All beside the point anyhow: UWF had already accepted me for *graduate* study in public administration the month *before* in *July!*

"The Admissions Committee of the **MPA** *program has decided to grant you full admission to the program for the Fall Quarter 1979...,"* wrote **Lynton R. Hayes**, Chairman, Political Science, UWF, in his acceptance letter dated 23 July 1979. *"We are looking forward to having you in the* **MPA** *program."*

"We are pleased to inform you that your application for admission to the above–named **graduate** *program has been approved for the quarter indicated...,"* wrote **Edith A. Cones**, UWF admissions director, in her acceptance letter dated 25 July 1979. *"We look forward to having you continue your education at The University of West Florida and wish you success in*

these endeavors."

"We are pleased to inform you that your application for admission to the above–named **graduate** *program has been approved for the quarter indicated...,"* wrote **Edith A. Cones**, UWF admissions director, in her next acceptance letter dated 9 March **1981**. *"We look forward to having you continue your education at The University of West Florida and wish you success in these endeavors."*

So Blockhead Bennett's phony second–bachelor's–degree pretext for refusing to process my financial aid application was at once superficial and spurious.

"On September 19, 1979," **Jerry L. Maygarden**, assistant vice president of Pensacola, Florida's now–defunct **Mutual Federal** savings and loan association, wrote to Blockhead Bennett in his letter dated 11 October 1979, obtained under the federal **Family Educational Rights and Privacy Act(the FERPA or Buckley Amendment, 1974)**, *"***Mutual Federal Savings and Loan Association** provided your office with notification that we were not engaged in processing a* **Federally Insured Student Loan** *application for Mr. Joseph Covino, Jr. Since that time, we received an application from Mr. Covino and notified your office of his request for a loan in the amount of $4,000. Following careful evaluation of Mr. Covino's application we have decided to reject the loan request. Please accept this letter as formal notification of our intentions."*

Lamebrain **Maygarden**, receiving from UWF a BA in 1974 and in 1975 an MA in "Communication Arts" and serving as *Student Government Association(SGA)* president(1974), was a university functionary and flunky from way back; so the scheming collusion of UWF's corrupt good old boy network was far–flung and far–reaching indeed!

"The financial aid office regrets to inform you they are unable to recommend another **Federal Insured Loan***,"* Bennett wrote in a curt and cryptic memo dated 6 February 1980 he sent me at the ***University of South Florida(USF)***in Tampa, where I'd taken another sabbatical during that winter quarter of 1980 to escape temporarily my Cuban–American harpy of a wife, Elizabeth, whom I was separating from.

Cryptic, I say, because of Blockhead Bennett's lame–ass, piss–poor attempt to disguise the fact that it was *HE* and he *alone*—not the "financial aid office" or some nebulous "they"—who outright refused to recommend for me the federally insured student loan I was perfectly eligible and qualified to receive.

"Should you require further information," Blockhead Bennett added arrogantly, knowing full well that I resided transiently across the state at ***USF*** in Tampa, Florida, *"please contact us for an appointment."*

To make a long story short, I'd met my Cuban–American harpy of a wife, Elizabeth, from our turbulent days together at *Florida Atlantic University(FAU)* in Boca Raton; we'd only been married since June 1978—after she'd been administratively booted out of *FAU* for her harmful emotional and mental problems—and had hardly even lived together for very long before first separating during the spring quarter of 1979; I returned temporarily to *FAU* and Elizabeth relocated to my backwater hometown of Pensacola, Florida to enroll at my alma mater, UWF—resorting to money I'd given her from funds I'd earned by teaching social studies at parochial high school in West Palm Beach, Florida during the fall and winter of 1979.

At Elizabeth's instigation we met up again and

lived together in the on–campus dormitories at UWF for the summer and fall quarters from June through December 1979. Throughout that time Elizabeth made my life a complete and utter misery. So out of sheer frustration I was forced to beat a most desperate but temporary retreat to the *University of South Florida(USF)*at Tampa for the winter quarter 1980.

What clueless Blockhead Bennett didn't know—before it was way too late for him to do a damn interfering thing about it—was that I forwarded the *Florida Guaranteed Student Loan(FGSL)*application his office certified to *Martha Mashburn*, EDP Specialist, *Florida Student Financial Assistance Commission(FSFAE)*, Insured Loans, who foresightfully got the loan financed for me through a bank in *Miami* rather than in Pensacola.

Even though it was awarded to attend a different university(*USF*)other than UWF, I out–maneuvered, out–smarted and out–witted Blockhead Bennett at his own conniving bureaucratic game, obtained the financial aid*(FGSL)*I was after all along—spending precious little of it at Tampa since I kept my expenses at *USF*, including classes, at a bare minimum—returning to UWF *on my own terms* within a single academic quarter by March 1980.

Even after returning to UWF for spring quarter 1980, I traveled to *USF* in Tampa to simultaneously register and withdraw from a bare minimum of classes to secure the substantial financial aid awarded me as well for that second spring quarter—retaining the remainder of that financial aid award*(FGSL)* to spend back at Pensacola attending UWF!

So despite Blockhead Bennett's meddling I'd received two out of the three *$834* installments of that *$2500* loan. And all I had to do for it was relocate temporarily to Tampa for a single 2–1/2–month quarter to regroup!

A clever and unconventional move on my part, for sure, but perfectly open and aboveboard—compelled by CR Bennett's bureaucratic chicanery.

Then I returned to UWF for the spring quarter 1980 with a *vengeance!*

Throughout that time my Cuban–American harpy of a wife, Elizabeth, and I both lived on–campus at UWF in separate private dormitory rooms until she'd depart altogether after graduating by August 1980— leaving me on my own to cavort on campus in unfettered peace and freedom!

Subsequently Blockhead Bennett would falsely accuse me of withholding from him information about my educational indebtedness—he left me no alternative—and enrolling in school for student loan deferments to evade making repayments on that educational indebtedness.

To recapitulate Blockhead Bennett's prejudiced and judgmental processing of my financial aid applications during this period:

•In August 1979 Blockhead Bennett refused without reason to release my processed *Federally Insured Student Loan(FISL)*application for *$4000* for graduate public administration studies submitted the previous June 1979—an entire two months before.

Because of my nebulous "prior educational indebtedness," Blockhead Bennett pompously presumed, Pensacola's local but now–defunct *Mutual Federal and Savings Loan Association* would "probably" reject my loan request: naturally, their official functionary and flunky, *Jerry L Maygarden*, controlled the funds!

It would be "highly unlikely," Blockhead Bennett

pompously presumed further, that the *Florida Guaranteed Student Loan(FGSL)*program would financially assist me either—even as a "lender of last resort."

Pretty preposterous a presumption because as we spoke—but unbeknownst to Blockhead Bennett—the *FGSL* program had already awarded me *$2500* to attend the *University of South Florida(USF)*in Tampa for the 1979–1980 academic year!

Previously the *FGSL* program had already awarded me *$1500* to attend *Florida Atlantic University(FAU)* in Boca Raton for the 1977–1978 academic year as well.

"The University of West Florida sent your application in to this office the end of last week," EDP Specialist, *Martha Mashburn*, *Florida Student Financial Assistance Commission(FSFAC)*, Insured Loans, notified me in her sympathetic letter dated 8 February 1980. *"They did not certify the application. I talked with* **Mr. Bennett** *at the University of West Florida and he would not recommend an amount. Until they do so, we can not process the application for you. I sent the application back to the school. This matter will have to be cleared up by you and the University of West Florida. This office can not solve the problem for you. I'm very sorry for the inconvenience."*

Blockhead Bennett outright refused to assist me because he pompously presumed likewise that I'd require upon graduation an employment position of a certain income–level—arbitrarily and capriciously preordained by him—to properly repay all my educational indebtedness.

Blockhead Bennett lamely endeavored to discourage me from even applying for student loans for *graduate* study, threatening to reduce in retaliation the undergraduate student loan and work–study financial aid benefits already awarded to my Cuban–American harpy of a wife, Elizabeth—on the unfounded presumption that I would automatically receive the *$4000* in proceeds from the *FISL* application he finally released to me since he somehow knew beforehand—likely through collusive communications with savings and loan functionaries(like *Jerry L Maygarden*)—that it would ultimately be rejected.

The subsequent *FISL* application Blockhead Bennett maliciously refused to certify for *Martha Mashburn* at the *FSFAC* was for just $834—the very same amount of my *FGSL* award installment for the spring quarter 1980 had I stayed in Tampa to study at *USF*—because he knew full well that if he did certify it that I'd most definitely receive it; later on that particular application mysteriously disappeared from my financial aid file altogether.

Well, I received most of that financial aid anyway—in spite of Blockhead Bennett's interfering intransigence—because I simply traveled to *USF* in Tampa to collect it!

Blockhead Bennett was subsequently force–fed my student loan deferment forms from *USF* to eat—doubtless making his blood boil!

"Please find enclosed," **Diane E. Moore**, *USF*'s assistant director, registrar's office, wrote me in her letter dated *25 April 1980* found in Blockhead Bennett's UWF financial aid file on me obtained under the federal *Family Educational Rights and Privacy Act(the FERPA or the Buckley Amendment, 1974)*, *"copies of the four subject forms which were completed and mailed as requested on February 14(to* **Wachovia Educational Services***–two forms), April*

*11(to University of West Florida)and April 25(original to **Wachovia**, a copy to UWF)."*

•Blockhead Bennett falsely claimed he had not received my *Financial Aid Form(FAF)*information from the *College Scholarship Service(CSS)*for the subsequent *FISL* application I submitted to his office for graduate studies for the 1980–1981 academic year— despite receipt of my *FAF*"acknowledgment" from the *CSS*(No. 5567557)displaying UWF as a recipient! So he sent me multiple "incomplete application" notices.

Blockhead Bennett went to any treacherous lengths to wrongfully prevent me from receiving student financial aid which I was perfectly eligible for and entitled to!

"You're wasting your time," Blockhead Bennett scoffed with a smug guffawing laugh by telephone long–distance Monday the 11th of February 1980 once I told him I'd submit complaints about his prejudiced and judgmental treatment of my financial aid applications to the US Department of Education.

"Oh, I'm interested in assisting *students*," Blockhead Bennett snidely cracked, insinuating that I wasn't a legitimate student.

Time would only tell who'd have the best, last and loudest laugh!

A single sheet of paper found in my UWF financial aid file dated "21 Sept 80"—obtained under the federal *Family Educational Rights and Privacy Act(the FERPA or the Buckley Amendment, 1974)*—contained this *hand–written* letter–draft signed by Blockhead(CR)Bennett:

"Program Review Officer, Lender Review Branch, Atlanta Regional Office, Dept. of Ed., called 18 Sept 80 regarding a letter from J. Covino to Washington that had been referred to them for action. A part of

his concern was an August incomplete application no-tice from the campus f.a. office indicating the need for an FAF. He had attached a CSS acknowledgment form listing UWF as an FAF recipient & dated Feb, 80. He is listed in our...inactive roster of 80–81. FAF files with a 20 Feb 80 process date. However, this of-fice has no record of receipt & after a careful check of student folders failed to locate it. Immediately after talking with the D. of Ed. regional office I personally called CSS in Princeton, N.J....& requested a dupli-cate copy of the complainant's FAF. Upon completion of the application process, Mr. Covino will be given full consideration depending upon the availability of...funds & full–time enrollment status in a program leading to a Master's in Public Admin."

It seems my complaints to the US Department of Education hadn't amounted to "wasting my time" after all—though a final–form draft of Blockhead Bennett's letter was conveniently missing from my student financial aid file. This was one thoroughly corrupt bastard!

"Copy of your Federally Insured Loan application(OE 1154)for the 1979/80 academic year is not complete," **Marion D. Watkins**, Program Officer, Lender & State Agency Branch, Division of Certification and Program Review, **United States Department of Education**, finally wrote me months later in her curt letter dated 20 October 1980, *"in that your loan history(which would have been on the back of the form)is not included. We did ask our contractor for a search of **FISL** commitments issued, however, and have determined that a **$2500** commitment was is-sued in August, 1979 for that same academic period. This prior commitment would account for the fact that a **$4000** loan for the same period would have been*

rejected, as the maximum loan amount would have been exceeded."

"As you indicated," **Marion D. Watkins** wrote me exactly one month later in her letter dated 20 November 1980, *"the school's portion on the part–copy of the 1154 received from you was completed. The* **lender***'s portion was incomplete. Regardless of the fact, however, that only part of the recorded commitment for the same school period had actually been disbursed, the record of the total amount committed would prevent the processing into the system of another application without subsequent corrections to override the system."*

"Written notices were mailed to you from this office on October 13, 1980, December 20, 1980, and January 19, 1981 concerning the **delinquent status** *of your* **National Defense Student Loan***,"* Clod **Charles E Clark**, university controller, wrote me in his letter dated 9 February 1981.

That bogus "delinquent status" of that **NDSL** was maliciously contrived from the start!

"Per your request dated February 6, 1981 accompanying a **Florida Guaranteed Student Loan** *application,"* Blockhead Bennett wrote me in his curt note dated 27 February 1981, exploiting the latest phony pretext UWF had fabricated to wrongfully deny me any financial aid, *"I provide this written explanation of my refusal to certify the form. You are in* **default** *on a* **National Direct Student Loan** *at the University of West Florida and therefore based on the statement you request I certify, you are ineligible for receipt of* **Guaranteed Student Loan** *funds."*

"Your request for a **$1,660 Federally Insured Student Loan***,"* Blockhead Bennett wrote me in his condescending note dated 2 March 1981, *"dat-*

ed January 16, 1980, covering the period 3/31/80 to 8/29/80 was denied because it conflicted with the loan period of a $2,500 FISL renewal with Southeast First National Bank of Miami processed through the Florida Student Financial Assistance Commission. This information would have been conveyed to you per instructions in a February 6, 1980 letter but you never requested an appointment."

Poor bitter, frustrated and petty sorehead, **BLOCK**–head Bennett—still grousing even at that late date because I'd made an utter fool of him by pulling that **FISL** over on him! Tough tittie, Blockhead Bennett!

To date repayment on my ditsy **National Direct Student Loan(NDSL)**dated 30 June 1976 had been duly delayed by legitimate student–deferments which Blockhead Bennett, in cahoots with other cohorts of UWF's corrupt good old boy network, were making in concert lame–ass, piss–poor attempts to wrongfully *retract—retroactively!*—conniving to revert me to "non–student status" to prevent me from registering for future classes, and to fabricate further pretext with which to evict me from on–campus residence.

*"The **Florida GSL** form you submitted February 6, 1981,"* Blockhead Bennett falsely claimed in his curt memo to me dated 28 July 1981, *"was voided because you were **at the time** in **default** on a **National Direct Student Loan** for attendance at The University of West Florida."*

"The University of West Florida financial aid office is unable to certify your **Florida Guaranteed Student Loan** application dated August 7, 1981," wrote Blockhead **CR Bennett**—by then re–born as phony–friendly **"Ray"** Bennett, *"because you are in default on a **Federally Insured Student Loan** for* *attendance here and utilized **FISL** funds from the **Bank of Pensacola**. Payment was due on the loan April 30, 1981, and was not received. Therefore, the bank has accelerated repayment of your loan and has filed a default claim with the Division of Claims and Collections, Office of Student Financial Assistance, Region IV(Atlanta), Department of Education.*

*"Your **$2500 Florida Guaranteed Student Loan** application for Fall Semester, 81, and Spring Semester, 82, with a Master of Public Administration major and a May, 82, graduation date, has been voided and will remain in your folder without financial aid office certification."*

§

Curiously contained in my official UWF student *financial aid file*—obtained under the federal ***Family Educational Rights and Privacy Act(FERPA, the Buckley Amendment, 1974)***—I discovered a ***letter–to–the–editor*** I'd written to the ***Voyager*** student newspaper dated ***9 August 1979***. Its closing excerpts:

*"Students refusing to be intimidated by UWF officialdom, their Ph.D's, administrative designators, and other titles of nobility can take heart in this comment by a prominent **Florida Atlantic University** professor of public administration:*

"'Many people are educated far beyond their intelligence,' he stated.

*"This writer could care less if the above–mentioned column("Across the President's Desk," by UWF president, **James A. Robinson**)was never printed again. In fact, it's a shame that the **Voyager** has become a puppet publication of UWF's administration.*

"Fortunately, times are changing. Many students, for instance, are no longer tolerating bullying by high and mighty professors, counselors, and administrators who know nothing but academic snobbery.

"No longer are many students passively accepting scornful badgering by faculty for legitimate tardiness and absence from classes which are very often useless and lacking in any substantive value.

"No longer are many students abiding by arbitrary, discretionary, and oppressive rules, regulations, and irresponsible and inflexible bureaucratic decisions.

"For UWF's officialdom, this message should be clear: students earn and pay for their education and degrees. UWF employees are paid only to serve—not harass—students.

"The best consolation for students suffering injustice at the hands of UWF's fat cats—those sitting pretty in their plush offices wielding what they think is unchecked power—is this:

"Those who knowingly and deliberately harm others will in the end be dealt with by a mortal and justice–bent life that has a natural and uncanny way of calling to account people indifferent to the misfortunes they cause their victims."

§

Blockhead Bennett was already keeping close and careful tabs on me even then. Be *afraid*, Blockhead Bennett. Be ***VERY*** *afraid!*

SIX:

PUTTING

THE

MONEY

SCREWS

ON,

PHILLIP M WALTRIP,

*COLLECTIONS
MANAGER*

T uesday the 20th of January 1981 UWF Collections Manager, *Phillip M Waltrip*, called me unexpectedly at my private on–campus dormitory to demand that I belatedly make not one but *four(4)*already student–deferred repayments on my minuscule *National Direct Student Loan(NDSL)*, threatening to place his shitty university's ominous and ubiquitous "hold" on my academic and registration records—effectively preventing me from enrolling in future classes and reverting me to "non–student" status—if I didn't pay up.

Ultimately UWF's corrupt good old boy network could connive to exploit that "non–student" status as a pretext to evict me from on–campus residence—at least that was their evil–minded, ill–intended but wishfully thinking design!

Even my private on–campus dormitory room telephone extension was supposed to be protected by formal privacy request.

Waltrip thought he was *so* cute though, conniving to circumvent that privacy protection by instructing the university switchboard operator simply to connect his call with my private dormitory room telephone extension—shared with three other privately residing students in that dormitory "suite"—and then asking anybody else except me who answered the telephone to tell him the extension number.

That privacy protection supposedly included not only your phone number but also your name, address, class and dates of university attendance.

So UWF switchboard operators—with the indulgent sanction of their indifferent supervisor, *Joseph Harper*—violated the spirit if not the letter of that privacy protection by indirectly and unduly divulging both your residence and attendance dates, since only currently–enrolled students could live on–campus!

It'd already come to my knowledge that that twerp, Waltrip, personally telephoned the editor of UWF's *Voyager* student newspaper, **Bill Fielding**, the previous fall quarter 1980, calling into question my right to submit for publication letters–to–the–editor—on the groundless pretext of my supposed "non–student status" when I temporarily withdrew from UWF but promptly pre–registered for the five–hour credit course(*INR 3006*)in which I was then currently enrolled. As if that student newspaper was never free to publish letters from readers who weren't actually students!

And so came to light that lame–ass, piss–poor attempt by a corrupt official of the *University of Worst Florida(UWF)*to outright *CENSOR* my First Amendment right of free speech and expression! I knew then for sure that I'd been doing something right!

A copy of Twerp Waltrip's hand–written and typed collections log was found in the *financial aid* file on me—obtained under the federal *Family Educational Rights and Privacy Act(the FERPA or the Buckley Amendment, 1974)*—proving that Blockhead *CR Bennett*, director, kept close and careful tabs on me throughout:

•*"8/7/79: 'Mr. Bennett asked that consider him a risk code 3 due to his conversation with Mr. Covino– per Phil.'*

•*"2/6/80: During week of 1/28/80, Ray(Blockhead Bennett)& I discussed file in depth–*

•*"1/20/81: 'Collection Manager telephoned Housing office to see if living on campus. They said they couldn't give dorm number or phone number due to privacy act–but agreed to transfer call to him. A man answered and said the extention number was 2011 when asked by collection Manager, he called out for Mr. Covino, and Mr. Covino answered him and said to ask who was calling, when he was told it was* **Phil Waltrip** *with the Controller's Office he directed the person to say 'tell him it's too early and he is not available right now.'(The time was 8:30a.m.)The collection manager then left his extention(sic)for Mr. Covino to return his call.*

•"1/20/81: Collection manager called Mr. Covino(11:30a.m.). Mr. Covino answered telephone when the collection manager told him who he was and he was calling about Mr. Covino's past due **N.D.S.L.** *account, Mr. Covino replied, 'I don't want to hear your mousey voice and don't ever call me again.' He then slammed the phone down.*

•"1/22/81: Collection manager began listing records and communications in Mr. Covino's file to discuss with **supervisor(Clod Clark)***for suggestions on how or what to do. Upon putting student deferments in order by dates, the collection manager noticed that there were some dates that overlapped with more than one college. Based on this information, he called the colleges in question and spoke to the records and registration office and found that Mr. Covino had received student deferments for* **three** *quarters that he wasn't eligible for this making him due* **$190.08** *for* **four** *quarters plus $19.08 collection cost, for a total of* **$209.08.** *It is also noted that there is a 'hold' on Mr. Covino's records for past due housing rent and an exit interview form he was supposed to submit for his N.D.S.L. account.*

"It should be noted that there has been considerable problems and collection activity with Mr. Covino

on past loans and bad checks–it is my impression that
he has had or is having similar problems with most if
not all of the colleges he has attended."

§

It should've come as no surprise to Twirp Waltrip,
not knowing me from Adam, that I'd experienced
"similar problems" elsewhere—as if my indigent condition was supposed to be some incriminating and
damning evidence of my deliberate "delinquency" and
"default."

What Twirp Waltrip conveniently neglected to
note was that I'd also told him that it would be simply
impossible for UWF to bleed me white!

The whole unadulterated truth of the matter was:
at that moment in time I was a 26–year–old kid—totally self–supporting since 17 without any financial
assistance from either family or friends—still strug-
gling to accomplish certain educational goals. At that
moment in time as well I was bicycling most every day
eight miles round–trip from the remote university
campus(inaccessible by public transit)to work regular
part–time(the euphemism for just short of full–time)
at a retail bookselling position at a shopping center
mall **four miles** distant from UWF. In the meantime
I was being hit up in divorce court for "alimony" by
my soon–to–be former Cuban–American harpy of a
wife, Elizabeth, who'd already fled home to mama in
Key West, Florida.

All beside the point in the end as Twirp Waltrip's
presumptuous and self–serving "impression" was
wholly wrong: out of one community college and not
one but **four** so–called "upper level" universities I'd
already attended, UWF was the one and **ONLY ONE**

worthless institution of **LOWER LEARNING** so actively, busily and maliciously engaged in instigating its campaign of debt–collection persecution against a single destitute student, owing—by Twirp Waltrip's clearly contrived account—a comparatively paltry debt of *$190.08!*

SEVEN:
PUTTING

THE

MONEY

SCREWS

ON,

CHARLES E CLARK,

CONTROLLER

"Your account of *$343.47* for a *National Direct Student Loan* is still outstanding and has now been turned over to our Collection Manager, *Phil Waltrip*," read the first notice from UWF Controller, *Charles E Clark*, dated 19 January 1981. "Please contact him before January 30, 1981 to avoid him having to take further steps to collect this long overdue account."

A copy of Clod Clark's initial letter was found in the *financial aid* file on me—obtained under the federal *Family Educational Rights and Privacy Act(the FERPA or the Buckley Amendment, 1974)*—proving that Blockhead *CR Bennett*, director, kept close and careful tabs on me throughout.

"Subsequent to the telephone call to you on January 20, 1981, a complete review was made of your NDSL file," Clod Clark wrote me unexpectedly in his letter dated 9 February 1981 just a fortnight later. *"During the review process, it was determined that you had submitted student deferment forms to the University of West Florida for the following periods of time for which you were not eligible for student deferment status...*

"Federal regulations require that a student must be enrolled at least half time(6 hours in undergraduate studies)to be eligible for student deferment status. Although the deferment forms were accepted by the University of West Florida for the periods specified above, you were not eligible for student deferment status. In accordance with federal regulations, you must now remit payments toward your NDSL balance for those specified periods of time.

"The official records of the University Registrar indicate that you are enrolled for five credit hours, INR

3006, *for the current quarter. Since you are not en-rolled in the minimum hours for student deferment status, you are not eligible for a student deferment for the current quarter...*

"Since you have not responded to previous efforts of this office to work with you to bring your account into a current status, I must establish a deadline of March 1, 1981 whereby you must remit the amount specified above to bring your account into a current status. If you fail to do so, the entire balance of your loan plus accrued interest and collection cost will become due in accordance with section III of the promissory note.

"A hold has been placed on your future registration and academic records until such time your accounts are brought to a current status."

Clod Clark copied this extortion letter to another cohort in UWF's corrupt good old boy network, student affairs vice president, **Kenneth L. Curtis**, who like UWF collections manager, **Phillip M Waltrip**, made lame–ass, piss–poor attempts to outright **CENSOR** my First Amendment rights of free speech and expression.

Clod Clark was deviously and maliciously reneg-ing—*retro–actively*—on not one but *four(4)*student deferments his shitty university had already duly ac-cepted, postponing previously due repayments on my minuscule **National Direct Student Loan(NDSL)** spanning the period from June 1978 through December 1980.

Clod Clark had the unmitigated temerity to charge me a per–deferment "Collection Cost" for each of the previously student–deferred **NDSL** repayments he was then trying to extort from me.

The bottom line: Clod Clark's evil–minded, ill–in-tent was to extort from me a grand total of *$256.60* by the 1st of March 1981 in their conspiratorial attempt to prevent me from registering for future classes and ultimately evict me from the UWF campus for reverting forcibly to "non–student" status.

Paranoid delusion? Hardly. Why else should I—of all students attending UWF, living on–campus and incurring such a minute indebtedness—be singled out so selectively for Clod Clark's "complete" and blatantly discriminatory "review?"

Significantly Clod Clark had doctored the student–deferred **NDSL** repayment for the 6/78–8/78 as being an **undergraduate** period for which I'd been enrolled for *five(5)*hours in course credit at **Florida Atlantic University**(where I was classified as a **graduate** student)in Boca Raton—when in actuality those had been **graduate** study credit hours.

HALF–time for **GRADUATE** study course work "in accordance with federal regulations" was then **4.5** hours—**NOT** the *six(6)*credit hours Clod Clark dubiously claimed, fabricating my **graduate** hours as **undergraduate** hours for that specific academic period.

"The enrollment requirements at both Florida Atlantic University and the University of West Florida are six quarter hours for undergraduate classification and five quarter hours for graduate classification," grudgingly confirmed **Thomas W. Henderson**, UWF business manager, in his more neutral letter dated 4 March 1981. *"We have contacted Florida Atlantic University and have been able to determine that you are in fact **eligible** for a student deferment for the period 6/78 to 8/78. The five hour undergraduate course you were enrolled in for during that time period qualifies you as a half–time student since you received **graduate** credit for the course."*

So I effectively struck down at least one of the four

false claims trumped up by UWF's corrupt good old boy network that my legitimate student–deferments for that ditsy **NDSL** were suddenly—and *retroactively*—invalid.

My last **Wachovia Services Inc.** account statement then indicated that my latest "deferment form has been received and processed," indicating that my next **$45.53** payment wasn't due until the 1st of **June** **1981** and that a **zero** amount outstanding balance was currently due on that account.

Paranoid delusion? Hardly. Why then did Clod Clark wait until that late date in February **1981** to dubiously claim that I was ineligible for student deferments from mid–**1978** through the end of **1980**?

"Mr. Covino," Clod Clark equivocated in reply in his condescending letter dated 18 February 1981— bureaucratic functionaries invariably start **Mister**– ing you as a prelude to talking **down** to you—*"based upon the tone and technical content of your letter, I do not feel it would be productive to engage in a series of letters to you to explain or justify the various operating procedures, rules and regulations, or points of law concerning your financial **obligations** with the University of West Florida."*

Nor concerning the University of Worst Florida's *"obligations"* to me as a student, evidently.

"I remind you that the hold remains on your academic records and future registrations at the University until such time your accounts are brought to a current status," Clod Clark closed his monotonously threatening extortion letter. *"The deadline date of March 1, 1981 specified in my letter of February 9, 1981 for bringing your **NDSL** account to a current status remains in effect."*

Clod Clark had me shivering in my shoes with

that letter!

Once more Clod Clark copied his extortion letter of 18 February 1981 to his collusive cohort in UWF's corrupt good old boy network, student affairs vice president, Clod **Kenneth L Curtis.**

All that over–complicated(if not convoluted) *QUIBBLING*—I've saved the best for last—was over my *National Direct Student Loan(NDSL)*to attend the *University of WORST Florida* dated 30 June 19**76**—and duly *DEFERRED* to date—in the *PIDDLING* amount of *$475!*

Imagine how many disadvantaged students at that time—in actual *"default"* on their student loans—must've been deeply indebted to UWF for literally *thousands* of dollars!

I had little alternative then except to raid my piggy bank(see *Chapter 14*)!

In person that Tuesday the 3rd of March 1981 I returned to the cashier's office at UWF to pay the *$47.53* the latest *Wachovia Services, Inc*. billing statement indicated that I owed as payment on that *NDSL* due March 1st(Sunday, a non–business day), pestering *Jacqueline T. Berger*, Fiscal Assistant Supervisor I, to explain away(in a tape–recorded conversation)the blatant discrepancy between that billing statement and Clod Clark's hyper–inflated outstanding claim of *$256.60* past due—*retro–actively* owing to four wrongfully cancelled student deferments.

Me: "Can anyone explain to me why *Wachovia Services* says I owe less than what UWF says I owe?"

Berger: "The deferment forms that were filed for four different quarters—that were outlined in one of the letters that you got—were certified for less than what they consider half–time."

Me: "But why doesn't *Wachovia Services* record

that?"

Berger: "They haven't been notified of it yet."

Me: "Why not?"

Berger: "Because it takes *six weeks* to update their records—they have been notified—they just haven't updated their billing yet."

Me: "Will they update it soon?"

Berger: "Yeah. It should be within *four or five weeks*."

Me: "*Four to five weeks?*"

Berger: "Yeah. Well, see, I said it takes *six weeks* from the time that we sent the letter to them. I can't remember if it's been one or two weeks since we sent the letter."

Why such a protracted delay?

Berger: "Because the company is a billing service for us, you know...We tell them what to do, therefore, we feel we're the *first authority*."

Yavo, Commandants!

In the meantime I contacted directly *Wachovia Services, Inc.*, the billing statement company administering my *NDSL* account, requesting that they reconcile the blatantly inconsistent discrepancies persisting between their billing statements and UWF's deliberately distorted(and overly inflated)invoices for the very same *NDSL* account.

Clod Clark imperiously instructed *Wachovia* representatives to outright refuse to cooperate with me or to communicate to me the reasons much less the rationalizations for those discrepancies.

"*I again*," *Kathy Riddle*, *Wachovia* Section Manager, wrote me in her brief letter dated 14 April 1981, "*contacted our customer, the University of West Florida concerning your account. I talked with Charles Clark, the Controller, on April 6th. Mr.*

Clark has instructed me to have you contact him as there is no information I can provide you with.

"Mr. Clark also stated that all future correspondence should be directed to him as he desires to handle this situation. Please understand that I am not evading your questions. West Florida is our customer and we must handle their accounts as we are instructed."

A polite and even sympathetic cop–out letting me know that **Big Brother** was in complete and total control!

"According to the records of this office," Clod Clark wrote me in his letter dated 9 June 1981, *"the University's invoice number **14246** submitted to you on June 1, 1981, is correct...*

*"As indicated on the University's cash receipt number **19951** dated March 3, 1981, the **$47.53** payment was applied to this past due charge, not the billing due on March 1, 1981 as stated in your letter.*

"In keeping with the University's policies, any payments are applied to the oldest charges first. Such was the case with your March 3, 1981 payment."

My "letter" simply re–stated the most current and up–to–date **Wachovia Services, Inc**. billing statement, which UWF deliberately disregarded.

It was the typical plot UWF hatched to perpetuate a distressed student's indebtedness indefinitely: artificially contrive a "past due" amount on the student's account—putting that account into arrears and rendering it "in default"—by improperly mis–applying the student's on–time payment on the current(and correct)outstanding balance against that artificially "delinquent" amount! All contrary to even the student's best intentions for making payment in full according to their own express purpose.

In effect, these UWF shysters and rip–off artists

imperiously dictate to students how, when and where to spend their own money!

"Since your accounts remain in a past due status," Clod Clark wrote in his deceitful letter dated 18 June 1981, *"I cannot remove the hold on your records to allow you to register for the summer quarter. As soon as your entire delinquent balances are paid in full, the hold will be removed from your records and future registrations at the University. I have discussed your account status with **Mr. T.W. Henderson**, University Business Manager, and he concurs with this decision."*

EIGHT:

PUTTING

THE

MONEY

SCREWS

ON,

KENNETH L CURTIS JR,

VICE PRESIDENT, STUDENT AFFAIRS

K*enneth L Curtis*, UWF student affairs vice president, imperiously proclaimed his dubious authority to "clear" for off–campus broadcast by *WSRE–TV 23*—the local *PBS* member station operated by *Pensacola Junior College(PJC)*—the *"Images and Reality in Education"* panel program, moderated by *Dr. Erskine S. Dottin* and videotaped in Studio B at UWF's Instructional Media Center the previous December 1980.

That six–student panel program centered round the question: *"Students at UWF: Are They Pawns In A Game Of Repressive Tolerance?"*

Because I myself actively participated in it, vociferously exposing UWF's rampant corrupt bureaucratic policies and practices, Clod Curtis quite naturally *CENSORED* that videotaped panel program from ever being broadcast by that local *PBS* station, which had indeed aspired to broadcast it.

Subsequently I would expose that shoddy episode of outright *CENSORSHIP* to both UWF's student government association and the *Northwest Florida Legislative Delegation*.

NINE:

PUTTING

THE

MONEY

SCREWS

ON,

THOMAS W HENDERSON,

BUSINESS MANAGER

Trumped up collection of my ditsy *$475 NDSL* ascended to the next higher–up in the upper echelons of the corrupt good old boy network hierarchy, ***Thomas W. Henderson, III***, who made his lame–ass, piss–poor attempts to explain away UWF's relentlessly deliberate and spiteful campaign of bureaucratic coercion, harassment, intimidation and extortion in my petty case!

*"At anytime a student's account is **referred** to the University Collection Manager for collection efforts,"* Harebrain Henderson claimed dubiously in his letter dated 4 March 1981, *"and where the debtor contests the charges, a complete, **routine** review of the student's file is made."*

Harebrain Henderson naturally neglected to name ***who*** precisely *"referred"* my account to the collection manager, ***Phillip M Waltrip***, a rancorous action—which was anything but *"routine"*—but which was doubtless deliberately instigated by Blockhead ***CR Bennett***, UWF financial aid director.

Like Clod UWF Controller, ***Charles E Clark***, before him Harebrain Henderson deliberately disregarded my request for an honest and straightforward explanation of the reason ***why*** their fraudulently finagled demand for *$209.08* in *retro–active* ***NDSL*** payments dated 9 February 1981 *preceded* by just *four* days the ***Wachovia Services Inc***. billing statement dated 13 February 1981 indicating the next installment payment of just *$47.53* due June 1st—as well as why the protracted delay to reconcile the blatant discrepancy between the last month–old ***Wachovia*** billing statement and the current *retro–active* charges artificially contrived by UWF designed to perpetuate my indebtedness.

"Since you were not enrolled in at least a half–time

study program for the summer quarter, 1981, you are not eligible for deferment for the period covered by this statement(June 1, 1981 through September 1, 1981)," Harebrain Henderson falsely claimed in his letter to me dated 23 September 1981. *"Your current enrollment at the University of West Florida and Pensacola Junior College combined possibly makes you eligible for student deferment status for the fall term, 1981... If payment...is remitted to the Cashier not later than September 28, 1981, I will not accelerate the balance of your NDSL account. If payment is not made on or before that date, the balance of your loan will be automatically accelerated and consideration will not be given to you for student deferment status for the fall term, 1981.*

"Your immediate attention to this matter is essential."

"Since you failed to meet two extended dates which I gave you to bring your account to a current status," Harebrain Henderson wrote me in his letter dated 29 September 1981, *"the remaining balance of your NDSL loan has been accelerated in accordance with the provisions of the promissory note...*

"Further, no consideration will now be given for student deferment status for the fall semester, 1981, for your enrollment at Pensacola Junior College or the University of West Florida. A permanent hold has been placed on your academic records and will remain there until the enclosed invoice is paid in full.

"If the remaining balance of your loan continues to be remain unpaid, an appropriate claim will be filed in the Escambia County Summary Claims Court.

"Your immediate attention to this matter is recommended."

TEN:
PUTTING

THE

MONEY

SCREWS

ON,

BILL M HUDNALL,
UWF HOUSING DIRECTOR

"*eference is made to your letter of January 24, 1981 to Mr. Phil Waltrip of my staff concerning the amount in which payments are applied to your housing rental account with the University,*" UWF Controller, **Charles E. Clark**, wrote me in his letter dated 2 February 1981, replying in the place of his ineffectual functionary, Twirp Waltrip, UWF's collections manager.

*"Please be advised that it is the policy of the University of West Florida to apply any payment made by **any** student, first to account balances owed in **arrears** and second, to accounts which are current. This policy is **consistently** applied to **all** students...*

"A hold is currently on your academic records and future registrations and will remain so until your accounts with the University are brought current."

A copy of Clod Clark's housing letter was found in the **financial aid** file on me—obtained under the federal **Family Educational Rights and Privacy Act(the FERPA or the Buckley Amendment, 1974)**—proving that Blockhead**(CR)Bennett**, director, kept close and careful tabs on me throughout.

"We do not send invoices for rent due, but do send them for late fees," **Bill Hudnall**, UWF housing director, wrote me in his condescending letter dated 9 February 1981. *"The responsibility for making the total rental payment, without penalty, is yours. After consultation with the University Controller(Clod Clark), it was pointed out that the policy of the University of West Florida is to apply any payment made by any student, first to account balances owed in arrears and then to accounts which are current. This policy is applied consistently to all students. All of our accounts are received and disbursed through*

the Controller's office, so the Housing office must and will support the current policy."

A copy of Dullard Hudnall's letter was found in the *financial aid* file on me—obtained under the federal *Family Educational Rights and Privacy Act(the FERPA or the Buckley Amendment, 1974)*—proving that Blockhead*(CR)Bennett*, director, kept close and careful tabs on me throughout.

All that to–do comes about whenever a student pays in good time their housing rent for the current month whilst owing an unpaid "late fee," so–called, for the previous month's late–paid housing rent.

So the housing office deviously deducts the previous month's "late fee" from the current month's rent payment, rendering the current rent payment "delinquent" and so technically "past due" as well—incurring yet an additional "late fee" and, as a consequence, perpetuating unduly(and artificially)the student resident's housing indebtedness!

Notwithstanding the fact that a "late fee" is not part of any "total *RENT* payment," Dullard Hudnall sorely needed to *TAKE* rather than lecture about "responsibility" for fair, honest, non–deceptive and good faith business dealings and practices!

"The Housing Office will not grant you permission to remain in campus housing as a non–student for the Spring Quarter, 1981," Dullard Hudnall wrote me in his curt "memorandum" dated 10 March 1981. *"Upon restoration of your student status, you may re–apply for campus housing."*

According to UWF rule, any lame–ass, piss–poor and petty attempt to louse up even my on–campus life.

"The contract and prepayment MUST be received by this date(June 1, 1981)for you to maintain your

present option," read a notice to private dormitory residents dated 15 May 1981 from **Frank Kelly**, UWF assistant housing director.

By accident or design the UWF housing office supposedly received my renewal contract the 2nd of July 1981—one month past the designated deadline.

"We are in receipt of your contract for on–campus housing," Dullard Hudnall wrote me in his memos dubiously dated 12 & 18 June 1981, acknowledging my renewal contract dated 6 July 1981 as a pretext of compelling me to suffer the inconvenience of moving across campus to a different private dormitory.

Specifically I was moved clear across campus from my long–time room 302 in Building 16 to Room 103 in Building 35—with the kindly help of my brotherly friend and long–time UWF maintenance man, **Mr. David Gant!**.

"The space which you currently occupy is unavailable to you because in order to maintain your priority you must have had your contract and prepayment submitted by June 1, 1981," wrote Dullard Hudnall's chief flunky, **William Murphy**, UWF assistant housing director, in his letter to me dated 6 August 1981. *"Your contract and prepayment were not received until July 2, 1981; therefore, your application was dropped from 1st priority to 2nd priority, and placed with other students in deposit date order.*

"It is not possible to give you the space you presently occupy because that space was assigned to another student before your contract was confirmed."

"You did not automatically lose your room because you did not pay by June 1, 1981," Dullard Hudnall equivocated in his memo to me dated 10 August 1981. *"You lost your room because a number of other people paid their money and submitted their contracts re-*

questing space in the 14, 15, and 16 cluster of build-ings before we received your contract and prepayment on July 2, 1981."

And so the petty and picayunish bureaucratic she-nanigans continued!

ELEVEN:

PUTTING

THE

MONEY

SCREWS

ON,

PHILLIP R. CAMPBELL,
ACADEMIC SERVICES
DIRECTOR,
UNIVERSITY REGISTRAR

"**M**r. *Joseph Covino, Jr.,*" wrote **Phillip R. Campbell**, UWF academic services director & registrar, wrote the **Guaranteed Student Loan Center** at **Wachovia Services, Inc.**, in his letter dated 10 September 1981, "*...is enrolled for 3 semester hours of undergraduate work at The University of West Florida. Although he has been accepted into the Graduate Program, he has not enrolled in any graduate courses.*

"*The formula that the State uses for full–time status is 12 semester hours for undergraduate status and 9 semester hours for graduate.*

"*For a student to receive Financial Aid at the University of West Florida, the present policy is 12 semester hours to be considered full–time undergraduate and 9 hours graduate.*

"*In Mr. Covino's case he is not considered half–time in that he is taking 3 semester hours...*"

TWELVE:

KICKING

THE

ENEMY'S

ASS

"Ihave contacted the controller at UWF,"* *Martin **Niforth**, Program Specialist, Division of Training & Dissemination, Student Financial Assistance, **United States Department of Education** first wrote me in his letter dated 30 March 1981, *"but without your permission, they will not speak to me concerning your loans. I am forwarding copies of your letters to Mr. Clark requesting that he handle your concerns and respond to me."*

§

"...if the lender has made satisfactory arrangements with a borrower to repay an NDSL then the borrower would not be considered in default at that institution," **Martin Niforth** *wrote me in his letter dated 3 June 1981. "In your case, the final determination of what constitutes a satisfactory arrangement of payment will be determined by Mr. Clark. This could be payment in full as it is in many institutions. If this is his rule, it must be the same for all defaulted borrowers and not just for you.*

"I have contacted the school requesting that the financial aid office coordinate its records with the decision made in the controller's office."

§

*"I have forwarded your June 12, 1981 letter concerning your 'Default Status' to Mr. **Charles E. Clark**, Controller at University of West Florida,"* **Martin Niforth** *wrote me succinctly but most gratifyingly in his note dated 29 June 1981. "I requested that he resolve this situation, reconcile your records at the school and* **Wachovia** *and respond to you and for-*

ward a copy to my office."

§

"*Regarding your inquiry into the default status of Joseph Covino, Jr.,*" wrote **CR Bennett**, UWF financial aid director, in his letter dated 11 June 1981 first responding to **Martin Niforth**, who was inquiring on my behalf, "*and its relationship to his **Guaranteed Student Loan** application request, he remains in default and has not made satisfactory arrangements to correct the condition. Despite what Mr. Covino stated in his May 20, 1981 addendum to a April 6, 1981 letter, he remains in default and will not receive financial aid office recommendation of a **GSL** as long as that condition persists...Mr. Covino...is not current and remains in default.*"

§

"*To confirm our telephone conversation of July 2, 1981, please be advised that Mr. Joseph Covino brought his **NDSL** account to a current status on June 22, 1981...,*" wrote **Charles E Clark**, UWF Controller, in his letter dated 7 July 1981 to **Martin Niforth**, who was inquiring on my behalf. "*He continues to be ineligible for student deferment status since he is enrolled for less than half–time status in undergraduate level course work.*"

§

"*The acceleration of your loan occurred after the deferment period began and therefore is invalid,*" **Martin Niforth** confirmed most gratifyingly in his letter to me dated 19 October 1981. "*I have instructed Mr. Charles Clark that because of the timing of the deferment period the acceleration **must be reversed***

*and **deferment granted**. Also the hold on your records must cease, if it is based on a defaulted **NDSL**.*

*"This reprieve from acceleration is based solely on
a technicality which Mr. Clark is appealing directly to
Washington..."*

§

*"I am enclosing a letter dated October 19, 1981
from Mr. **Martin Niforth** of the Region IV Office in
Atlanta,"* wrote **Charles E Clark**, UWF Controller,
in a long–winded three–page letter dated 27 October
1981 to **Margaret Henry**, Acting Branch Chief,
Campus Base Programs Branch, Division of Policy and
Program Development, **United States Department
of Education** in Washington, DC, *"concerning the
acceleration of the **NDSL** loan account of Mr. Joseph
Covino, a student enrolled at the University of West
Florida. According to Mr. **Niforth**'s letter, the
University of West Florida has **improperly accelerated** the balance of Mr. Covino's **NDSL** account with
the University.*

*"In order for your office to better understand the
actions taken by the University, some background information on this particular account is essential.*

*"Mr. Covino's account has a long established his-
tory of default, refusal to pay installments when due,
holds on academic records and the like...*

*"**Mr. Niforth** refers to Section 674.34 of the
January 19, 1981 Federal Register as being the section of the **regulations violated** by the University of
West Florida in the acceleration of Mr. Covino's **NDSL**
account...*

*"This letter is written as a **formal appeal** of the in-
terpretation of the regulations as cited by **Mr. Martin
Niforth** in his letter of October 19, 1981. It also serves*

as a follow up to our telephone conversations on the matter.

"The rescinding of the acceleration of Mr. Covino's account and the release of the hold on his academic records and future registration at the University of West Florida is being held in abeyance until such time that a final ruling on the issue is rendered by your office.

"I look forward to hearing from you soon."

§

*"This is to confirm our conversation of March 2 regarding the **NDSL** account of Joseph Covino,"* wrote **Margaret O. Henry**, Chief, Policy Section, Campus–based Branch Division of Policy and Program Development, Office of Student Financial Assistance, Office of Postsecondary Education, **U.S. Department of Education**, in her letter dated 4 March 1982 to UWF "Comptroller," Clod **Charles E. Clark**, *"From the information provided by the University of West Florida, the institution **will have to accept the deferment form** submitted by Mr. Covino for course work at Pensacola Junior College. The institution can, of course, accelerate the loan, should the borrower fail to meet the next scheduled repayment."*

Will **"HAVE"** to accept! **SWEET!** What beautiful bureaucratic music to my ears that single, solitary, heartening, gratifying, exhilarating, welcome and wonderful phrase! For once—for a change!—UWF's corrupt good old boy network was dictated to, ordered and **compelled** by higher–ups(at *my* instigation!)to do something they literally loathed against their will and wishes!

§

"I am enclosing a copy of a letter dated March 4, 1982, from the U.S. Office of Education wherein **Ms. Margaret Henry** *states that the University of West Florida* **must accept the student deferment form** *submitted by you and received by this office on October 7, 1981,"* Clod **Charles E. Clark**, UWF Controller, who was finally compelled to grudgingly concede beautiful bureaucratic **DEFEAT**, wrote me in his letter dated 8 March 1982. *"Therefore, I have placed you in a student deferment status, retro–active, for the period August 24, 1981, through December 11, 1981. In addition, the action taken by the University on September 29, 1981, to accelerate the balance of your* **NDSL** *loan has been* **rescinded retro–active** *to September 29, 1981.*

"Your next installment on your **NDSL** *loan account was due on March 1, 1981...*

"Failure to submit either an executed student deferment form or payment remittance for the March 1, 1982, quarterly billing will result in the balance of your loan being declared immediately due and payable without further notice to you."

Bitter, bitter SOUR GRAPES!

Roughly a year earlier, UWF financial aid director, Blockhead**(CR)Bennett**, scoffing and guffawing, told me I was "wasting(my)time" making administrative appeals to the US Education department.

Guess who was **LAUGHING** quite heartily then? To this day I'm **STILL** laughing about it—*and* him!

THIRTEEN:

CLOD

CLARK'S

BIG

LIE

"In response to your September 10, 1981 letter concerning your federally insured student loan at the **Bank of Pensacola**," Clod **Charles E. Clark**, UWF controller falsely assured me in his letter dated 14 September 1981, "the answer is **no**. I have **not** and **will not** place a hold on your record concerning this loan since it is with a private banking institution rather than the University of West Florida."

Like most unscrupulous bureaucratic officials in UWF's corrupt good old boy network, Clod Clark was and is an out and out **LIAR!**

"It has been verified with the U.S. Education Office in Atlanta, Georgia," Clod Clark wrote me, expressing a drastic change–of–**black**–heart in his pretext letter dated 14 June 1988, "that you are in default on a Guaranteed Student Loan issued to you by the **Bank of Pensacola** while attending the University of West Florida...

"Pursuant to Federal and State regulatory require-ments, a **hold** has been placed on your academic re-cords at the University of West Florida. That hold must remain on your academic record, which includes the release of academic transcripts, until such time that the University of West Florida has been notified by the U.S. Education Office in Atlanta that you have satisfied the obligations of that loan."

"In response to your letter of March 2," witless **James Witt**, UWF political science department chair-man wrote me in his letter dated 13 March 1989, "be advised that you will not be able to matriculate at The University of West Florida until your problems with the U.S. Education Office have been resolved. Enclosed you will find a copy of a letter(Clod Clark's) sent to you on June 14, 1988, which stated our initial *position that has not changed."*

"In response to your letter of January 10, 1990," **Patricia J. Whitfield**, UWF records & registration director, wrote me in her letter dated 19 January 19**90**, *"this office is unable to fulfill your request for transcripts **because you have a financial obligation to The University."***

The unadulterated truth of the matter was and is: I didn't then and haven't since owed that utterly worthless university a damn dime!

Nor had I the slightest desire or intention to ever "matriculate" back to worthless UWF for yet another worthless degree of whatever grade!

Those oh–so–*formidable* UWF files, records(including "academic transcripts")and holds— or so the chumps comprising UWF's corrupt good old boy network most mistakenly think!

To this day—nearly **40 YEARS** hence—I've never, ever had *any* cause to request the first worthless transcript record from worthless UWF for *any* purpose!

Except of course just to *test* the records hold status.

FOURTEEN:

THE

PENNIES

EPISODE

*"It's too bad there aren't **thousands** of Joe Covinos," UWF cashier's office customer, quoted by **Gus Harris, 30 March 1981***

Now *this* was *real FUN!*

Together with a girlfriend witness and armed with a running miniature tape–recorder, I went on the warpath Monday the 23rd of February 1981 ready to most indignantly confront and defy in his own knavish den of iniquity(the cashier office)UWF controller, *Charles E Clark* himself!

Me(9:08AM): "I would like to know how much money *exactly*—how much money that I owe the university on my *National Direct Student Loan*."

Cashier: "All right. Let me see if I can locate your file and I'll be right back."

Me: "Very well."

Clerk: "Mr. Clark has your file and he said the best thing to do would be to set up an appointment with his secretary and he'd be able to go over it."

Me: "No. I don't want to go over it. I want to know how much I owe—right *now*—so that I can *pay* it."

Clerk: "Well, all I can say is: go in there 'cause he has the file on his desk."

Me: "You're *refusing* to tell me how much money I owe the university?"

Clerk: "I am unable to because I don't have access to the file."

Me: "You don't have *access* to the file?"

Clerk: "That's right. He has it."

Me: "Is Mr. Clark *refusing* to tell me how much money I owe the university?"

Clerk: "He would like to have an appointment set up so that he can explain it to you."

Me: "No. I need to know—*now*—how much money I owe."

Clerk: "Well, maybe he has time now to go over it."

Me: "Well, I'm waiting..."

Clerk: "Well, ask the cash—"

Me: "No. I don't need to ask the cashier. I'm waiting here to know how much I owe the university. And I want to know *now*. There's no reason you can't tell me. Is there any reason?"

Clerk: "I do not have access—"

Me: "Well, tell Mr. Clark to tell me. I need to know."

Clerk: "Tell his secretary, please. I don't have anything to do with his—you know—schedules or anything like that."

Me: "Well, you can relay a message to Mr. Clark: that I am waiting here to know how much I owe the university. And I want to know how much I owe so that I may *pay*. And I'm waiting for an answer."

Clerk: "Okay. Hold on just a second and I'll see what the secretary..."

Clerk: "She says all that she can do is set up an appointment. He's in his office but he's busy today— or right now anyway—but she can set up an appointment for you."

Me: "You mean you people cannot...You people have written me in the mail and have told me I owe you hundreds of dollars—and you cannot tell me the exact amount that I owe the university when I come here to *pay*?"

Clerk: "Mr. Clark can, yes."

Me: "Then why can't he tell me *now*? Why can't someone tell me *now*?"

Clerk: "Go *ask* him."

Me: "No. *You* go ask him. I'm the customer. You are the public servant here."

Clerk: "Sir, I have done everything that I can possibly..."

Me: "And this is a public institution. And I am not

your servant. You are *mine.* My tax dollars subsidize *your* salary."

Me: "I still haven't had an answer to my question: how much money I owe the university on my **National Direct Student Loan**. Apparently, the cashier's office *refuses* to give me the information."

Clark: "Mr. Covino?"

Me: "Yes, I am."

Clark(shaking a pencil, eraser end up, next to his face, behind his glass–box cage): "I wrote you a letter and told you you could set up an appointment with me..."

Me: "Don't point your pencil at me, sir."

Clark(stubbornly shaking his pencil albeit with conspicuously restrained vigor): "I'm not pointing a pencil at you. I wrote you a letter and asked you to set an appointment—and that's the way you're going to *have* to do it. Okay?"

Me: "No. I don't *have* to do anything."

Clark: "If you're going to talk to me that's the way you're...Make an appointment with my secretary and I'll review your file."

Me: "I want to know: all I want is the amount— I don't want a review. I want to know—*now*—how much I owe you. And that's *it!*"

Clark: "Well, what do you plan to do if I tell you that?"

Me: "I'm going to *pay* you."

Clark: "Very good. I'll give you..."

Me: "I want the exact amount. *Now.*"

Clark: "In full. And I'll give you a statement to that effect. It'll take a few minutes to work it up."

Me: "Play games..."

Clark: "Sir?"

Me: "Do you wish to play games? I'm here to play

107

games."

Clark: "I'm not playing games."

Me: "Well, give me the amount then."

Clark: "Well, it's going to take a few minutes to work it up. I just don't go in there and walk in and hand you..."

Me: "All right. There's no need for an appointment then. Let's *do* it!"

Clark: "Okay. Well, it's going to take a few minutes. Do you want to wait?"

Me: "I'll wait."

Clark: "Okay."

Me: "I'm waiting. I've *been* waiting."

Clark: "Very good. And I'll have it for you in just a few minutes. Okay?"

Clark(9:23AM): "There you go."

Me(examining invoice): "I have another question for you, sir. Oh, it's gone *up!* If all of these fees are paid will the hold be removed from my records?"

Clark: "Yes, sir, it will."

Me: "Now in your records—that I obtained from your office—there's a note by someone—the author is anonymous—and it says that a hold was placed on my records partly because I didn't fill out some required exit interview form."

Clark(like a friggin' parrot): "That's right. That's right."

Me: "Will that still be in effect?"

Clark: "Not since you're back in school. There's no point in your filling it out as long as you're here now. If you depart the University of West Florida again you will need to fill one out."

Me: "Of course. Nowhere in the promissory note is that form required. Now—"

Clark: "Well, I'm not going to debate the regulation."

Me: "I don't want to debate. I just want an answer."

Clark: "It is required when you separate from the university."

Me: "By who?"

Clark: "It is an exit interview required. It's required by the federal regulations."

Me: "By federal regulations?"

Clark: "That's correct."

Me: "And that's a condition of my loan?"

Clark: "That's a condition of your separation and your NDSL loan. That's correct."

Me: "And you have the authority—you claim—to hold my registration records?"

Clark: "I certainly do."

Me: "If I don't fill out that exit interview form?"

Clark: "That's correct."

Me: "All right, sir. Thank you for your time."

Clark: "You're quite welcome."

Well, I never did fill out that so–called "exit interview" form.

Right there and then though I unexpectedly produced and presented to Clod Clark *four* bulging cloth bank bags—each one containing precisely ***$52.27*** apiece in ***pennies*** for a total of ***$209.08***—the outstanding balance due owing on my ***NDSL*** account!

Together with my girlfriend witness we made our discreet but hasty exit, *bursting with laughter!*

§

The ***UWF Keystone Cops*** "Miscellaneous Activity" report(***Case No. 810150***)on the incident read as follows:

109

"At appx. 0945 this date(2/23/81)Mr. Charles Clark called this office requesting the University investigator to come to the Cashier's Office. Upon my arrival Mr. Clark met me at the Teller's Window and showed me 4 bank bags which he stated contained a reported $209.08 in pennies. Mr. Clark advised that the money had been received from Mr. Joseph Covino, a U.W.F. student, for payment of a debt that Mr. Covino owed the University. Mr. Clark also stated that the bags which were sealed at the top with rubber bands had not been opened and that the amount of money Mr. Covino stated to be contained therein had not been counted and verified. Mr. Clark asked that U.W.F.P.D. take possession of the money at which time I advised him that since no criminal act had taken place and due to lack of storage facilities it would not be possible for me to accept the bags and money.

"Mr. Clark further advised me that pennies are not considered as legal tender for payment of a debt and I requested that he take this matter up with the University Collections Dept. I did witness the sealing of each bank bag by Mr. Clark who then placed each of the 4 bags in a deposit box inside the safe in the Cashier's Office. At the time Mr. Clark closed the safe I checked it for security and placed evidence tape across the locking mechanism and from the door to the side of the deposit box so that the box could not be opened without breaking the seal. I advised Mr. Clark to contact me before reopening the deposit box so that I could check the..."

§

"This is to officially advise you that the four bags of coins which you left in the University Cashier's of-

fice on the morning of February 23, 1981 are not acceptable as payment toward accounts owed by you to the University," Clod Clark wrote me in rejection in his rambling two–page letter dated that very same day. *"I call your attention to Title 31, Section 460 of the **United States Code**, which states that 'the minor coins of the United States shall be a legal tender, at their nominal value for any amount not exceeding **25 cents** in any one payment.' A copy of that section of the U.S. Code is provided for your reference.*

"The four bags of coins said to contain $209.08 in pennies was immediately sealed in the presence of Mr. Dick Granson, Campus Investigator, and were placed in the University vault under his seal. You may claim these four bags of coins at the University Cashier's Office between the hours of 8:15a.m. and 3:30p.m., Monday through Friday.

"No receipt is being written, your accounts are not being credited, and the hold on your records is not being released since legal tender payment has not been made by you..."

§

Right off I wondered whether the malarkey Clod Clark wrote about "legal tender" was valid since he quoted from the rather dated *1976* edition of the U.S. Code. But I ultimately decided to reclaim the coins all the same—especially since my ploy to get the pennies transaction photographed and written up in the campus UWF *Voyager* student newspaper had fallen through; the current reactionary university administration lackey–editor deemed it un–newsworthy as if it were a common, ordinary everyday occurrence! *Dipshit!*

I was already on shaky financial ground anyway.

So I simply cashed the coins in the 2nd of March 1981 at the local *Barnett Bank*, which simply poured the coins into a spinning, stainless steel–looking coin counter machine and returned to me exactly *$209.06*—just *two cents* short of the amount of pennies I'd first purchased at nearby *West Florida Bank*.

I'd proved my point—badgering and inconveniencing them as they'd done to me—and had a little blast doing it, mightily embarrassing Clod Clark in front of his entire staff in the process!

To this day I still **LAUGH** heartily at the humorously nervous, scared and worried expressions Clod Clark conspicuously displayed throughout that early morning encounter!

It likewise proved that UWF functionaries were far more interested in bureaucratically harassing and hounding me than in collecting payment on any debt.

§

The *UWF Keystone Cops* "Continuation Report"(*Case No. 810150*)on the incident read as follows:

"At appx. 1455 hrs. this date(3/2/81)this office received a call from Mr. Charles Clark at the Cashier's Office stating that Mr. Joseph Covino was presently at that location to pick up the bags of coins he had previously left there.

"Upon arrival at Bldg. 20E I met Mr. Chas. Clark and Mr. Gerry Norris and went to the safe with them and checked the seal I had placed on the safe deposit box which was holding Mr. Covino's money. The box had been sealed on 2/23/81. After inspecting the seal I had placed on the safe deposit box door and being satisfied that the seal had not been tampered with or broken I advised Mr. Norris that he could now break the seal and open the box. Mr. Norris opened the box in my presence and that of Mr. Clark and removed the contents which consisted solely of the 4 bank bags delivered to the Cashier's Office by Mr. Covino on 2/23/81. The seals placed on the bank bags were also still in place.

"Mr. Clark and Mr. Norris then delivered the bank bags to the Teller's window and handed them over to Mr. Joseph Covino who accepted them and left."

FIFTEEN:

UWF'S

KEYSTONE

COPS

"According to Ms. Covino he intended to drop out @ **South Fla.** and arrive back @ UWF sometime around 2:45am Friday morning. His intentions @ that time are not really known," **Sgt. W.H. Mixon**, **UWF Keystone Cop**, wrote ominously in his "Miscellaneous Activity" report dated late Wednesday night the 9th of January 1980 in response to a false complaint filed on–campus by my Cuban–American harpy of a wife, Elizabeth.

"He" referred to me, and my perfectly full "intentions"—to travel from Tampa to visit her in Pensacola, not "drop out" from enrollment at the **University of South Florida(USF)**—were clearly known to Elizabeth, who meant merely to scandalize me at UWF. Come Friday the 11th of January visit Elizabeth I would—and indeed with her perfectly free and willing consent.

Because I telephoned her that night in a distraught state—upset at being separated from her—Elizabeth exploited the predicament in her pathetic attempt to make me look like a crazed nut–case!

Jumping presumptuously to rash conclusions, Mixon, relaying his supposedly menacing message through Elizabeth, threatened to dispatch the Pensacola Police to intercept me at the downtown *Greyhound Lines* common carrier bus station or arrest me if I set foot on UWF campus. Mixon telephoned Elizabeth the very next day, interrogating her about whether I was showing up at Pensacola.

Elizabeth told Mixon absolutely nothing and by Friday the 11th I was wildly humping her again in her private dormitory room!

Of all the Keystone Cops on UWF campus that Mixon pig was the only one who outright refused to permit me to practice my trumpet after hours in the so–called commons or music buildings without a "special pass."

Despite her deceptively demure demeanor Elizabeth was the true emotionally disturbed and unstable mental case. She's primarily the reason why we ultimately divorced.

Initially Elizabeth attended spring quarter at UWF in March 1979 solely due to my own good offices, exploiting most of my separation pay from my parochial high school social studies teaching position in West Palm Beach to transfer from *Florida Atlantic University(FAU)*in Boca Raton—from which *she*(not me)had been compulsorily *expelled* for *her* psychological problems!

Excerpts from *FAU Campus Security Police Department "Incident Report"(Case Number: 78 0858)*"details" dated 21 February 1978:

"2345hrs, Off. Kiefer went into the ladies rest room near office, walked in the door noticed a large amount of dried blood approx. 1–1/2' wide on the floor in front of the sink, more blood on the door...went into the rest room upstairs, also a large amount of blood on the walls and the floor..."

Excerpts from *FAU Campus Security Police Department "Supplementary Report"(Case Number: 78 0858)*by Police Officer Kathleen M. Carson #13 dated 22 February 1978:

"0925 hours: BRCH(Boca Raton Community Hospital)contacted this station with regard to information on(Elizabeth). Spokesperson for the Hospital stated that(Elizabeth)had slashed both of her wrists, which confirmed an earlier comment of..., who stated that(Elizabeth)had cut both wrists with what was 'probably a blade.'"

Whilst teaching parochial high school social studies during the winter quarter of 1979, I personally employed West Palm Beach, Florida attorney, **Burton G. Sharff**, to officially protest Elizabeth's compulsory expulsion from FAU.

"Please be advised that this office represents Elizabeth...," Sharff wrote in his legal letter dated 9 February 1979 to **Karl F. Ijams**, FAU's student affairs dean. *"Our client advises that in April, 1978, she requested a medical withdrawal from **Florida Atlantic University** and now she has been **refused readmittance**. She has explained to me that there was a suicide attempt by her on February 21, 1978, and that she has been **refused admittance** until she receives outside counseling."*

"I have recently spoken with the attorney who represents Florida Atlantic University," Sharff wrote Elizabeth in his legal letter dated 13 March 1979. *"He informs me that the **Stipulation** for your **readmittance** is that you counsel with their staff **psychologist**...He tells me that this counselling must continue until you are released by the school **psychologist**, or outside counselor."*

Were it not for my support—like it or not—Elizabeth would've never been able(or capable)of even enrolling at the *University of West Florida(UWF)* for the spring quarter in March 1979!

SIXTEEN:

TC

COMMITTE,

CULPRIT

&

TRAITOR

The very first time I got rancid wind of pompous, pipe–puffing *Thomas("Dr. Tom")C.
Committe*(one–time chairman of UWF's finance and accounting department)was late
Wednesday night the 17th of December 1980 on–campus in Building 58 where I witnessed first–hand a
group of Chinese students, recruited by Committe to
work like migrants—sweat shop–style(albeit air–con-
ditioned)—in a mass–production, human assembly
line hand–addressing(now get *THIS!*)literally *hundreds* of personal ***Christmas cards*** from Committe's
extravagantly extensive list! Utterly unbelievable!

Committe, you see, was supposedly the great self–
appointed champion and paternalistic(translation:
pretentious)mentor of UWF's Chinese student community! Yeah, right!

§

Unbeknownst to the stupid chumps comprising UWF's corrupt good old boy network I'd already
taken up with a warmly caring and loving young
on–campus Chinese girl from *Taiwan*(formerly
Formosa)aka the *Republic of China(ROC)*, named
Shih–Tseng*(nicknamed "Alice"), months* before
since December 19*79!*—months before even my im-
pending divorce from my Cuban–American harpy of
a wife, Elizabeth, was finalized in early April 19*81!*
Throughout that time Alice had been my closest and
dearest—but secret—friend, companion and most in-
timate confidant. She had lent me both herself and
her aid, generously giving me both moral and mate-
rial support as well as boundless encouragement in
everything I did—including rebelling against revolt-
ing UWF! Even during my absence during the winter 1980 quarter—whilst I was transiently relocated

to *USF* in Tampa, Florida—Alice remained at–large on–campus at UWF as my private and special agent–of–assistance: filing paperwork, making payments, keeping me posted about all developments, everything!

By late September 19*80* Alice would have to enlist my tangible aid once she learned that one *James I Miklovich*, head of UWF's foreign exchange student program, suddenly sprung the not–so–good news that Chinese students were magnanimously granted tuition scholarships for just *three* quarter terms and that they were abruptly—and inexplicably—required to enroll for *20* quarter hours(as a compulsory condition of receiving any further funds)to complete their academic programs within just *two* more quarters.

So by August 1981 we were married and by October 1981—at her instigation—we freely and willingly left UWF campus of our own accord and—at our own pleasure—relocated to a private apartment complex in the east side of town near *Pensacola Junior College*. Once Alice simply applied for resident alien status in the states she'd pay just affordable in–state fees for college or university like all "bona fide" Florida residents!

UWF dean *RC Einbecker*, most disappointingly, pretended that he was powerless to help.

As did the great supposed self–appointed and oh–so–sage guardian of UWF's pacifistic Chinese community, *"Dr. Tom" Carrol Committe!*

Then several months later Friday the 19th of March 19*82* Clod *Charles E Clark*, UWF's controller, went through the wasted rigmarole of filing a lawsuit against us in the summary claims division of Escambia County court for the paltry outstanding balances on two of my UWF accounts: *$121.84(NDSL* loan)and *$230*(private dorm housing rent)—but most insidiously of all *$810.04* owing on Alice's so–called "short–term loan" account.

Insidious because Alice never owed UWF a damn cent of that cash: **Dr. Thomas("Tom")Carrol Committe**—the great self–appointed fatherly advisor and benefactor of UWF's Chinese community—had personally loaned her that money(*$800*)—out of his own pocket—to help her defray tuition costs for a previous quarter of study at UWF!

Committe let the UWF controller administer the loan solely to avoid the appearance of playing favorites to any particular Chinese student. Committe nevertheless promised Alice verbally that she could repay him the personal loan at any time as she was able—**without penalty**—if for any reason she could not meet the official UWF–administered loan repayment deadline of 31 December 19*81*.

Committe confronted Clod Clark, who admitted that he'd vindictively instigated that petty lawsuit strictly out of bitter exasperation and resentment because I'd made such a monkey of him by triumphantly deferring repayment on my **NDSL** account after my successful appeals to the **US Education Department**.

What had Blockhead*(CR)Bennett*, UWF's financial aid director, cracked so sarcastically—that I'd be *"wasting(my)time?"*

Well, when the chips were down and push came to shove, **Dr. Thomas("Tom")Carrol Committe**—the great self–appointed paternal sage Chinese champion—chickened out and buried his hypocritical head in the sand by refusing outright to officially go to bat for Alice! That bastard actually acted put–out that I'd asked him to stick up for her.

Had Committe had the balls not to cop out I'd been more than ready and willing to go to trial to expose UWF's disgraceful and blatantly discriminatory court action against innocent Alice—the gentlest, sweetest and most sensitive of souls who'd never harmed anyone or anything in her entire life.

Alice had knocked herself out, riding a rickety moped across town over dangerous roads(lacking politically correct bike paths)to hostess for some six months at *Peking Garden* Chinese restaurant(7751 N Davis Highway), earning her sizable savings for transferring to *Florida State University* in Tallahassee to study.

Long story short, Alice paid off in full—in one fell swoop—all our outstanding debts to be done with UWF once and for all time. Still I insisted that we pay solely the exact amounts I owed absent any so-called "late fees": *$115.84($6 less* than sued for on the *NDSL* account), *$220($10 less* than sued for on the student housing account).

We were *still* heartily *laughing* at Clod Clark and the rest of his affiliated buffoons because we'd also stuck them with all that wasted time and effort of filling out official court forms—and letters written canceling the discriminatory court action—as well as paying *$24* in court costs and *$12* in sheriff's service fees!

We'd made monkeys of the fools all over again!

PART II:

ARTICLES

&

SPEECHES

*"**Covino**(bless his little cherubic heart)is still carrying on in the empty footprints of the late great **C.A. Jimenez**"—**Patrick D'Amico**, letter–to–the–editor, **Voyager***

*"*he University of West Florida epitomizes the insensitivity and inflexibility
of bureaucracies generally. The consequences of administrative decisions
on individuals—the students who earn and pay for
their degrees—are blatantly ignored, deliberately.
Individual circumstances, situations, and feelings are
glossed over, paid scant consideration. Examples:*

*"•the college recently established a writing skills
proficiency requirement which all students must meet
before graduating—a problem which should be ad-
dressed at the grade school level, instead of burden-
ing hard–working college students with an additional
hindrance.*

*"•farcical counselors, like autocrats, have the au-
thority to plan undergraduate programs for students
in excess of the minimums listed in the UWF college
catalog—thus having the dictator–like power to extend, unchecked, a student's degree requirements indefinitely, at whim.*

*"•so–called $50 in late and reinstatement fees,
charges those students who pay their fees late, through
no fault of their own(unless being poor in financial
resources is a fault), hurting those students with the
least ability to pay, and in the most need of assistance.*

*"•unreasonable professors, who have the power to
deny, across the board, any make–up examinations,
no matter what circumstances befall a student—and
then requiring extra difficult and comprehensive final
exams.*

*"The endless list of inefficiencies and outright stu-
pidities go on and on. And some put–up, silver spoon–
fed, or bribed indigent student will answer this letter.*

*"But while students are treated like administrative
pawns, instead of human beings, it is most assuredly*

no surprise that UWF's drop in enrollment ranks a proud second highest in the state of Florida amongst state universities."
Thursday, 18 November 1976

§

The *STRANGE CASE* of *HUEY L LATHAM*

Huey L Latham, Jr was an incredibly starchy and self–conscious middle–aged economics instructor who sported gold neck–chains and colored '70s print shirts laid open to expose rather repugnantly his graying blond chest hairs! Curiously contained in my official UWF student affairs vice president file— obtained under the federal **Family Educational Rights and Privacy Act(FERPA, the Buckley Amendment, 1974)**—I discovered this special contribution I wrote for the **Voyager** student newspaper dated **23 October 1980**. Reproduced in its entirety:

§

Student's problem linked to UWF educator

"Another student earning and buying mediocre–quality education has been unduly victimized by UWF's typically underhanded administration.

"Larry Platte got from UWF's deplorable academic appeal system what, in his case, would be understatedly called the 'shaft.'

*"Instructor **Huey Latham**, however, was probably more responsible than the so–called Academic Review Committee—the token appeal board designed to preserve shoddy teaching and abused grading discre-*

tion—for Platte's problem.

*"As an economics major during the **1975–76** academic year, this writer successfully endured three quarters of classroom gloom under Mr. Latham's mock tutelage.*

"Students never speak or discuss knowledge in Mr. Latham's dismal classes.

"Facing Mr. Latham's overbearing arrogance and impatience with questions, his students are cheerless and somber.

"Mr. Latham tries intimidating any student disagreeing with the cynical, disparaging worldview he presents as academic instruction.

"Complaining about everything, while confusing his constantly pessimistic convictions with edification, Mr. Latham offers solutions to nothing. His students, meanwhile, pay tuition fees to subject themselves to a continuously opinionated bombast.

*"Examples quoted in a complaint letter I filed with UWF pres. Robinson in **August 1976** follow:*

"Congressmen are 'idiots.'

"'We are still a small, dumb nation. Did you know this?'

"Social security bureaucracy 'epitomizes inefficiency.'

"'The whole damn thing(the Vietnam war)was a fiasco.'

"'Politics(in research)has a tendency to screw up a lot of things.'

"Lemonade 'packaging is a bunch of crap.'

"'University committee meetings are 'reminiscent of ring–around–the–rosie. These are supposed to be academic people.'

"Congress is 'irresponsible as far as fiscal matters are concerned.'

"George Meany 'is an honest man. Let me rephrase that: at least he hasn't been caught at anything.'

"While teaching, Mr. Latham often requires his students—undoubtedly as a time–consuming measure—to write in their notes voluminous lists of dictated statistical economic data.

"He initially tells his students that the 'figures' are for their personal edification only—and then tests students on exams for rote memorization of the statistics given.

"When poor test grades result, Mr. Latham glibly sermonizes: students 'should study **all** their notes and not try to skip others.'

"After failing to distribute a course syllabus for an entire quarter, Mr. Latham blames 'the secretary.'

"He informs class latecomers that students already present received ten points for writing on paper their name and the course title.

"Administering his final exam on the last day of classes, Mr. Latham sardonically confronts his students with: 'We aren't going to go around talking about our final exam early, are we? If we do, we will have a **second** test on the test date first designated(on the university calendar).'

"He remarks to a shy girl giving a class presentation on how 'different it is to be in **front** of the class' rather than in it.

"He condemns newspapers while admitting never reading them.

"Examples abound where Mr. Latham fails to qualify his frivolous statements as opinion. Typifying Mr. Latham's sad classes, one student, while explaining to the instructor why he had failed to answer aloud a proposed economic calculation, perfectly summarized the prevailing mood: 'I was **afraid** to.'

*"When **fear** dominates a classroom, can Larry Platte or anyone else really be expected to learn much of anything?"*

§

Acting, self–appointed apologist for Latham, **Ron Miller**, UWF english department, pitched a temper tantrum–bitch in the **Voyager** student newspaper:

Enough from Covino

"All right. Enough is enough.

*"As a fairly sympathetic faculty member, I make a point of reading through the **Voyager** every week. I look to note the latest flap over Student Government, check to see what shows and lectures are coming up, skim the sports pages to find names I recognize, check the articles for illiteracies to exhibit in my writing classes, and glance at the classified section to see your generation publicly advertising for living situations my generation wouldn't have dared to practice secretly. But most of all, I pore over the editorial pages to see what students are thinking about at the moment.*

*"So this week I flipped open my **Voyager** to discover **TWO(2)**lengthy pieces by **Joe Covino**. Now, Mr. Covino's initial published temper tantrums were a bit of fun. Where else could one find the depth of thought of Charlie Reese wedded to the subtlety of language of the Voice of the Klan? Since Mr. Covino's worldview comes straight out of the sixties, being battered by his agitprop was at first a nostalgic experience, like watching **Hair** or not buying grapes. Then Mr. Covino turned vicious, launching personal attacks on individuals in a setting where the victim could not possibly defend themselves. Whatever the techni-*

cal justice or injustice of the situations discussed, the methods used in the cheap–shot assault on Professor Latham were those of poison pen letter and the obscene phone call. Freedom of speech and freedom of the press, I sometimes believe, are not the last but the very first refuge of the demagogue and the scoundrel. I naturally looked to the editors and faculty advisors of the **Voyager** *to exercise a bit of professional discretion and spare us the embarrassing aspect of Mr. Covino's continued adolescence. No such luck, no such professionalism. What* **is** *taught in journalism today? Scrounging up copy?*

"Anyway, worse than viciousness in the long run is dullness. By now we all know what Mr. Covino thinks. He's as predictable as Reverend Falwell or the Albanian government. By now he's worn out his whole bag of cliches. What possible good can be served by dedicating the most valuable sections of your paper to one more item of clinical evidence for his egomania and his hatred of authority? At some point even the most tolerant master of ceremonies gets the abusive drunk off stage.

"Come on: let us know what other students think. You discredit your needed role as critic of the establishment by making your dissent seem like nothing but the private writings of a disturbed individual. If you continue to fill your pages with Mr. Covino's self–indulgencies, in order to find out what is going on I will be forced to read the **Fountain***, with its unending list of faculty visits to the Rotary Club, instead. Please spare me that."*

§

Public Address to the UWF Student Government Association(SGA), Wednesday, 28 January 1981

*"Mr. President, Mr. Vice President and Members of Student Government, I am **very** grateful and honored for having this opportunity to address you.*

*"As you may or may not agree the **University of West Florida** both fears and stifles free and open debate of controversial subjects concerning the university.*

*"Last fall quarter 1980 UWF collections manager, **Phillip M Waltrip**, using the pretext of my 'non-student status' for the last few weeks of the term—when I temporarily withdrew from school—pressured editor, **Bill Fielding**, to censor my letters and contributions to the **Voyager** student newspaper.*

*"Likewise last quarter the UWF administration banned from off–campus broadcast a videotaped educational forum entitled, **'Students at UWF: Are They Pawns in a Game of Repressive Tolerance?'***

*"In that program UWF professor **Erskine S. Dottin** moderated discussion among five student panelists, including myself and your own executive officers, **Ron VanHorn** and **Dan Costello**.*

*"Notified later of the forum taping, **Bill Fielding** apparently decided against post–news coverage of the campus–related dialogue.*

*"The **Pensacola News–Journal**, at the same time, publishes little which opposes UWF. By reserving most of its editorial space for community elites, based on their economic, political or social standing, it limits access to its opinion pages mostly to a select group of business people, educators and politicians.*

*"The **UWF Foundation**, probably seeking influential supporters for the university expansion drive, published **Pensacola News–Journal** editor **J Earle Bowden**'s personal memoir, **Always the Rivers Flow**, all proceeds going to the Foundation publications and scholarships funds.*

"*As far back as* 1976 **Mutual Federal Savings and Loan Association** *Chairman and former* **Florida Board of Regents** *member,* **EW Hopkins**, *literally raved to me that, regarding personal academic appeals which passed even the highest university level,* **'I don't get paid a damn dime to listen to you.'**

"*UWF Arts and Sciences dean* **Lucius F Ellsworth**, *that same year, jeeringly assured me that he was 'eager' for even a legal confrontation over personal academic appeals.*

"*UWF financial aid director,* **CR Bennett**, *more recently, scoffingly told me that I was 'wasting(my)time' trying to secure impartial, independent third–party intervention, by outside regulatory agencies, in complaint matters involving UWF.*

"*Such brazen restrictions on free expression are simply intolerable in a free democratic society. So it is against this backdrop of administrative repression, callous indifference and pompous arrogance, that I reject censorship and eagerly address you.*

"*Concerning myself, I am twice a graduate of both* **Pensacola Junior College** *and the University of West Florida. I have successfully earned more than* **100** *semester and quarter academic credits from each school respectively.*

"*In academic specialty my four undergraduate degrees from these two schools range from economics, criminal justice and political science to international studies.*

"*I give you this information, not to boast, but to show through term of residence, that I have personally experienced UWF in a wide variety of ways—and that I have first–hand knowledge of its workings.*

"*My aim is not to degrade UWF, its personnel, or to*

use this respectable forum as a platform from which to air personal grievances against the university. Instead my purpose is three–fold:

"First, I want to inform you of my perceptions of some of the most subtle and yet some of the most detestable abuses ever committed against students by a university of its kind.

"Second, I wish to share my beliefs as to the real motives behind university expansion proposals and their implications for disadvantaged and minority students.

"Finally I hope to suggest areas needing reform and recommend solutions to particular problems and possible courses of action.

"Certain university policies and practices undoubtedly have dire consequences for students in terms of their extremely harmful effects on individuals—often in violation of their basic freedoms, equality, personal security and well–being.

"These are the students you never hear about—the ones who never make newspaper headlines.

"So if my presentation seems long it is only because the list of repulsive injuries inflicted on students by the university is equally long. If I sometimes speak bluntly it is only because the human damages done by the university are clearly depraved—and deserve the most forceful condemnation possible.

"I certainly have nothing to gain personally from this talk but probable scorn and personal ridicule.

"But I assure you I will not be discouraged by misguided people who believe censorship is the best way to handle controversy. I will always speak out for what I believe wherever I go—regardless of the consequences. It is certainly everyone's right to do so.

"In asking for your close attention, however, I ap-

peal for your open–mindedness, patience, tolerance and most importantly your careful and serious consideration of the crucial questions I set before you.

"Above all I implore you to respond to the issues with reason before emotion, with thoughtfulness before hasty disregard—and with action before neglect.

"For conquering apathy and encouraging greater student participation and involvement in matters affecting us all will best be accomplished, not by contempt of each other, but by our honest care, cooperation and sincere example.

"During the 1973–1974 academic year I served as Student Public Defender, a Student Government position, for PJC. So I can really identify with many of the problems you face while holding office.

"From that experience, however, I concluded that Student Government is mostly a symbolic and token body—being mainly an educational showpiece. It is not, in other words, a viable or an effective interest group. It certainly is not a political pressure group— though it should and could be.

"That opinion does not reflect badly on you. Most of us probably realize that real decision–making authority is concentrated in positions held by just a few university bureaucrats and technocrats.

"The effectiveness and success of Student Government, on the other hand, are very limited in terms of what it can actually accomplish.

"This does not mean that you accomplish nothing. Your record in achieving goals related to non–controversial projects is surely admirable.

"In its present form, however, especially with respect to changing established university policies, practices and procedures Student Government can achieve little or nothing.

"Your organization, amounting to government in name only, becomes as a result little more than a pretentious ritual.

"You cannot be blamed, however, for a situation which is not a fault of your own making.

"The university is simply not held accountable for serving or neglecting student needs and wants. It frequently acts capriciously against valid student concerns and interests—however defined—just as ruthlessly as it ignores student expectations and aspirations for self–serving ends.

*"As **Ralph Nader** often states: universities generally, while kow–towing to commercial and political interests, try to keep students disorganized by prolonging their adolescence into their twenties.*

"To be sure, far too many unjust university actions and practices go unchecked and unchallenged. Apathy is indeed your greatest enemy. But students need not stay disunited.

"UWF enrollment was estimated in 1967 to peak at about 13,000 students. Last April 1980, however, slightly more than 5000 students attended UWF. Despite continued and misleading boasts of record high enrollments UWF reached only one–third of its projected enrollment in 1979. Even if current enrollment is the highest number since UWF opened in 1967 the figures fall far short of enrollment projections and planning. This fact partly explains UWF's rush to add a lower division which will compensate for over–staffing and under–using its faculty because of exaggerated enrollment projections.

"During the next 20 years, predicts the Carnegie Council on Policy Studies in Higher Education, college enrollment nationwide will probably shrink 5 to 15 percent. So most colleges face the prospect of losing

students and funds in coming years if they fail to tailor their services to student desires.

"The obvious implication is: the time is right for increased student activism, involvement and participation in decisions affecting students' educational careers.

"A purpose of this talk is not to malign UWF but rather to encourage more student participation in university affairs.

"As you can well imagine I have been both cajoled and coerced from many sides to censor myself. I have been accused, among other things, of being 'radical.' I have been the subject of malicious gossip and petty rumor–mongering—all hazards of the muckraking trade, I suppose.

"People of dubious morality have tried—under the feeble guise of what they call 'compromise'—to persuade me to sacrifice convictions and principles for the sake of expediency. The so–called 'gray areas' of good and bad have been redundantly preached to me.

"As trite or as outdated as it may sound to you my intent is quite simple: to seek truth, justice and help people fight against every form and degree of tyranny. I ask no one to like or accept my methods.

"No one, of course, monopolizes truth or wisdom. But each of us must live according to how we each define them—and express ourselves consistently with our honest beliefs. When we share those beliefs among ourselves, hopefully, we find more agreement than conflict.

"Still, disagreement is never a sound justification for censorship. If we smother controversial dialogue here we only legitimize and support abuses the university wants to hide. If we silence free and open debate we only perpetuate the crimes we deplore. And if jus-

tice–seeking is a 'radical' enterprise then I make no apology for it.

"Although I confess to a strongly liberal outlook— which is my natural bias—I refuse to waste whatever integrity I do have for the sake of cheap expediency and foul neglect.

"Perhaps you feel I have little or no integrity— which is certainly your prerogative. But the subject of this address is not me but UWF. So I will finally come directly to the point:

"The University of West Florida is academically and administratively the most oppressive, money–voracious, morally corrupt and unresponsive of any school I have ever attended!

"Including UWF I have attended five different colleges or universities—four of which were Florida schools.

"To me public authorities exist to serve—not rule— their public clientele. Public institutions, likewise, exist to service—not subjugate—their paying customers. Students ought to be treated like adults and not subjects. They are, after all, consumers who earn and pay for the education they obtain.

"Public servants, as far as possible, should oblige the needs and wishes of their patrons. Public policies and procedures, to the greatest possible extent, should be naturally biased and weighted in favor of and not against the public served.

"Help–minded assistance is scarce at UWF. Hindrance is the rule—not the exception.

"The saddest tragedy of UWF is that too many students passively accept the injustices they endure. Too many, for whatever reason, fail to object to the abuses they suffer. Here are some examples:

"Academic Advising. *The UWF catalog, which*

Arts and Sciences Dean, **Lucius F Ellsworth,** *brags 'is not a contract,' reads that: 'The counselor has the authority to plan a program for a student in excess of the minimums(degree requirements)listed.'*

"Assigned and unsolicited academic counselors have the excessive discretion to literally hold student graduations hostage by forcing students to enroll—at an unnecessary waste of time, effort and money—for more courses than minimally required by either specific academic departments or the university itself.

"Economics instructor, Janet S Miller, has said that bypassing academic advisors in course scheduling makes 'a farce' of the counseling process—hard doing since the system was farcical from its inception.

"The effect is that so-called counselors can prolong student graduations indefinitely and at whim— despite the financial hardship or emotional anxiety caused students in the process. Degree planning sheets are not worth the paper they are written on.

"Obligatory academic advising should be outlawed. Counseling should be a voluntary, not a compulsory process. UWF counselors are not merely available to students. They are, instead, imposed on students—a situation which amounts to academic coercion for students unwilling to enroll for unrequired courses dictated to them by counselors.

"What's worse: most UWF counselors delude themselves into believing that doctoral degrees qualify them to give students 'paternalistic' and unsolicited advice on everything from personal problems to private future plans.

"But it is highly doubtful students attend UWF seeking surrogate parents.

*"***Literacy Test.*** Meddling in educational responsibility best handled at the pre-secondary level UWF*

*burdens hard–working degree candidates with yet an-
other graduation obstacle—its own version of Florida's
'literacy skills' test. If would–be graduates fail this
ridiculous and academically irrelevant test six times
UWF bilks them of more time, effort and money by
denying them their just due degrees until they complete a UWF remedial English course. Claiming the
need for remedial education for some UWF students
merely provides the university with another sly revenue source. In addition the test needs to be examined
for cultural bias.*

*"**Record Holds**. UWF, as a standard practice,
wrests student compliance with its verbal and written edicts by threatening the following: 'A hold has
been placed on all your records. This means that you
will not be able to register for any subsequent quarter,
you will not receive a transcript, which is your official
grade, and you will not receive a diploma until this
obligation is cleared.' The so–called 'obligation'—often a library fine or traffic ticket—usually amounts to
a petty debt. More often the 'hold' is typically a pretext
for UWF officials to force students to do their whimsical bidding.*

*"**Wage Garnishment**. The UWF collections manager high–handedly withholds work–study paychecks
of indebted students until—under duress—they agree
to sign over their pay to the university for debt–payment deductions. Under this practice UWF presumes
to order students to spend their own earnings in preordained ways.*

*"**Cashier Office Irregularities**. If a UWF private dorm resident promptly pays rent for one month
but is unable to pay a formerly assessed $10 'late fee'
from a previous month the university cashier deducts
the past 'late fee' from the student's current rent pay-*

ment. In effect the student's rent payment is automatically rendered insufficient to cover the current month's rent. The UWF cashier—after perpetuating the student's housing debt—then assesses the student with yet another 'late fee.' Even when students clearly designate on their payment instrument—whether check or money order—that the payment is to be applied toward housing rent—the cashier audaciously pre–decrees how students must spend their money.

"The cashier also charges students who, for whatever reason, pay their tuition late, up to $50 in so–called 'late and reinstatement' fees. The UWF registrar, meanwhile, automatically deletes from class registration lists the names of students who miss tuition payment deadlines—thus canceling out any completed course work for the term involved.

"Inanely the cashier refuses to let students owing UWF the puniest amount of outstanding debt to even pay for pre–registered classes. Again if registered students—as a result of the tuition payment prohibition—miss tuition payment deadlines and are assessed late fees UWF itself perpetuates student debt—and ultimately ensures itself of a calculated revenue source which is gotten at the expense of the university's neediest students.

*"**Housing**. Late rent penalties are unequally imposed and inconsistently administered. Punitive $10 housing late fees are imposed only on some but not all private dorm residents paying rent late. The policy, originating from the UWF cashier, is blatantly discriminatory.*

"The housing office now requires students to notify UWF of housing contract cancellations a full five days before students can officially withdraw from UWF with an automatic 'W' grade—generating, naturally,

more $50 cancellation fee revenue from students who might withdraw after learning their mid–term grades. To illustrate: the UWF housing winter quarter 1981 contract cancellation deadline for students not re- turning spring quarter 1981 is February 15. The last day to withdraw from a course or the university with an automatic 'W' grade for winter quarter 1981 is February 20.

"Most recently the housing office deleted from hous- ing contracts provisions confirming university hous- ing contracts for new students 'no later than 30 days prior to the entering quarter.' Incoming UWF stu- dents, then, have less than a month in which to make transition plans based on the indefinite availability of on–campus shelter.

"Housing contracts offer students no tenant rights and assume virtually no university responsibilities. UWF police, maintenance and other personnel can make abrupt 'pass key' incursions into student rooms 'yet the university is not liable for loss or damage of personal property or failure of utilities.'

"One UWF resident assistant informed me recently that UWF police actually 'harass' students they label 'criminal' as a means of letting them know that 'they are not welcome here.'

*"**Financial Aid**. Rather than helping needy stu- dents to the maximum extent possible, reports finan- cial aid officer Sarah Fortino, the UWF financial aid office now acts as a 'screening' agency for banks, sav- ings and loan associations and other lending institu- tions that finance government insured student loans. UWF financial aid—instead of the lending agencies themselves—decides which students are good credit risks. The office, in effect, judges which students are even worthy of receiving student loans. Its loopholed*

credit worthiness criteria checklist gives the financial aid director lopsided discretion in determining which students are even eligible to receive loan funds.

*"UWF financial aid director, **CR Bennett**, even brags that criteria his office uses in deciding how to disburse short–term emergency loans to penniless students are comparable to even the most generous private sector, commercial banking standards used under similar circumstances.*

"Is it any surprise then that UWF public safety and security department investigator, Wes Cummings, has admitted before that almost all previous campus assaults have related to contacts between students and UWF personnel?

"The catalog of UWF student abuses easily continues. Academic snobbery and overbearing impudence among UWF faculty—exhibited by their largely condescending attitude toward students—are rampant in student–faculty relations.

*"When a student crushed with personal tragedy lays bare every dreadful detail of an agonizing experience UWF counseling center director, **James R Holmes**, typically responds with the heartless remark: 'Well, no one ever said the world was fair.' Let us all hope that Mr Holmes is immune to personal calamity so that he will never be overwhelmed by another person's compassion.*

"Sometimes the brazen high and mightiness of certain base people is severe enough to infuriate even the most tolerant of individuals. But one of the most abominable crimes ever perpetuated against human beings by UWF is its victimization of Chinese students.

"It is a tragic outrage that many UWF Chinese students will return to their homeland with an image of America formed of maltreatment and neglect. For

UWF has typically deceived, coerced and degraded its Chinese community.

*"UWF business dean, **Richard C Einbecker**, earnestly promised a group of Chinese accounting majors, for instance, that 'tuition waiver' scholarships would be available to them for as many quarters as needed for graduation.*

*"Assuming control of the foreign student exchange program, however, UWF professor **James I Miklovich** now threatens to terminate current tuition waivers for Chinese students justly refusing to sign written 'understandings' limiting their UWF studies to just three full–time quarters.*

*"Similarly UWF foreign student advisor, **Mamette Byrkit**, haughtily threatens to 'hold' university records of Chinese students declining to spend their money on student health insurance or on an unnecessary, unrequired $258 English pronunciation course.*

"Byrkit, who brazenly advocates lowering the number of UWF Chinese students at university committee meetings, insolently admonishes new Chinese students lacking transportation to 'walk' to faraway banks, supermarkets and other suppliers of basic needs and services.

"Revoltingly Byrkit flippantly told one group of Chinese students wanting transportation help in making rotational visits to a hospitalized friend that walking was their only choice.

*"Over last Christmas break a group of Chinese students patiently waited nearly three full hours for a substitute driver to van them to **University Mall** for shopping when, without notice, the original driver failed to show.*

"Ali, the regular driver, is an ill–mannered boor who routinely threatens to leave stranded Chinese

students who are just five minutes late for departure times.

*"He once dropped one Chinese girl wanting to stop at nearby **Woolco Plaza** at **West Florida Hospital**— smartly telling her she deserved to walk across busy Davis Highway since she regularly objects to his characteristic rudeness.*

"Without doubt arrogance, indifference and intimidation are bizarre ways of fostering international friendship and understanding.

"And UWF—while exploiting the overtly passive nature of our kind Chinese neighbors—ought to account for its use or misuse—of the $60,000 student exchange grant it recently got from Nationalist China.

"Perhaps these episodes show how very little influence UWF students actually have on administrative and academic policy.

"I now ask you: whose interests do you really serve? Your own? Those of the university? Or those of the larger student community whose interests you were elected to promote? Or even perhaps a combination of these?

"Foremost on your list of priorities, I believe, should be your representation of student interests.

"But how effective can you be when you share little or no decision–making authority with the UWF administration? Patronizing it will not achieve substantial changes in the problems just described.

"Perhaps a new approach to your official duties might be driven by a critical attitude based on clearly defined values and carefully developed priorities.

"As an important tool of analysis the logic behind university policies and practices can be examined and constantly reviewed. The underlying assumptions of many university procedures, you may find, are often

faulty and invalid. Many low–income students simply unable to pay all their university debts on time, for example, are automatically assumed by UWF officials to be scheming connivers who deliberately evade their obligations.

"Sometimes our wider loyalties to community, state, country and even to the world may surpass those of self and the university. An increase in our regressive state sales tax—to the benefit of education, for in-stance—would burden poor citizens to a much greater degree than it would affect rich people.

"Issue analysis can be undertaken with a broader and more far–sighted perspective than which occurs now.

"Amid the university expansion debate, for exam-ple, the values most often stressed are economic de-velopment, national prestige and student exclusivity formed of an elite student body.

"Preferred values, however, might include increased educational quality, equal access to educational op-portunity and improved administrative responsive-ness to student needs and wants.

"Proposed are new structures for redressing student grievances against UWF:

•Complaint Committee. An independent stu-dent investigative panel that—with the consent of the complainants—publishes its factual findings in the Voyager newspaper.

•Civil Lawsuit Fund. Money specially earmarked for students needing lawyers to sue UWF over proven university abuses.

•Whistleblowing Committee. An indepen-dent investigative panel that collects and publishes evidence of university abuse, mis–management and waste given by secret informants recruited by publicity

from the ranks of the student body and even university personnel.

"Your choice now is simple: you may act or react. You may respond to student apathy with frustration and indifference. Or you may initiate system reform.

"Change certainly will not come easy or lack personal sacrifice. The resolve to act ultimately rests— not with the UWF student body—but with you. The question now is: are you willing to meet the challenge?

"Thank you for your time and forbearance."

§

Public Address to the Florida Legislative Delegation, Thursday, 29 January 1981 (Published in the Voyager, Monday, 9 February 1981)

"Mr Chairman. Members of the Delegation. Concerned citizens.

"Concerning the question of whether the University of West Florida should add a lower division of freshmen and sophomores, thereby becoming a four–year university, some lawmakers have recently suggested publicly that nothing more on the issue needs to be debated or discussed.

"They are dreadfully wrong.

"Our local newspaper, especially, fails to responsibly publicize all the relevant information and dialogue regarding expansion controversy.

"The sad truth is: the most vital questions involving university expansion have been callously and blatantly ignored if not altogether suppressed.

"During the university expansion debate, for instance, the goals most often stressed and publicized are economic development and growth, national uni-

versity prestige based on prominence in research or varsity sports, not to mention an elite and exclusive student body gotten at the expense of our community's less endowed students.

"These are, perhaps, laudable goals having both dubious methods and deplorable effects.

*"Expansion backers wish to accomplish their self–serving ends by literally destroying the life of **Pensacola Junior College** and by attracting to UWF the so–called 'brighter' students of our state.*

"This is not the best way to prevent the so–called 'brain drain' from Florida universities. Perhaps free college tuition for state residents would be a more appropriate measure.

*"Expansion supporters scheme to relegate the functions of **Pensacola Junior College** to providing merely adult, remedial and vocational education.*

"They heartlessly plan to deny students, which they high–handedly label "marginal," access to an upper-level education. Their nefarious device of student exclusion is the elitist and academically irrelevant admissions test.

"When university expansion proponents defend tougher admissions requirements they really mean higher test score achievement. When they speak of upgrading educational quality they really mean turning away students whom they audaciously judge to be undeserving of a higher education.

"UWF, I believe, is part of a collusive scheme connived by business people, educrats and politicians to form an exclusive labor pool with which to attract more industry to Florida.

*"The question is: should this be the highest mission of—not only UWF—but of **any** university?*

"UWF in addition desires to compensate itself for

151

over–staffing and under–using its faculty because of errors in exaggerated enrollment projections based on little more than wishful thinking.

"Their strategy consists of stealing students and funds from community colleges, private schools and even rival four–year institutions.

"The immediate results of university expansion are well recognized: duplicated educational services, higher consumer costs due to higher university faculty salaries, increased university administrative and support personnel, and inflated tuition fees. This amounts to tax dollar wastefulness.

"The more detestable and long–term effect of university expansion is to deny equal educational access in our community to those so–called "marginal" students who may perform badly on the one–shot, high–pressure situation of a culturally biased admissions test—or who may lack the mobility or income to seek education elsewhere.

"While university professors emphasize research and publishing for the sake of prestige only bad teaching and inferior research can result. Superior teaching and research simply cannot be undertaken by single professors at the same time.

*"How can anyone use economic development as a justification for denying students equal educational access, or making education more expensive for consumers and voters, when the total number of students as a result of university expansion would be merely shifted from **Pensacola Junior College** to the university?*

"The university expansion concept literally reeks of discrimination against low–income and minority students.

"Parents of college–age students having disadvan-

taged backgrounds should be outraged at the expansion proposal. And if they knew the reality they probably would be.

*"The **Florida Board of Regents 1979** consultants' report was supposed to answer the question: what **kind** of students would be eligible to attend universities which expand?*

"That crucial matter has been maliciously ignored by the local mass media and the so–called powers–that–be.

"Enrollment in two–year community colleges jumped from 2.2 million in 1970 to more than 4 million in 1978. Costs at these schools are typically less than half that of average four–year institutions.

*"The **US Department of Education** reports that university enrollment nationwide is peaking this year and will fall steadily for the rest of the 1980s.*

*"During the next 20 years, predicts the **Carnegie Council on Policy Studies in Higher Education**, university enrollment nationally will probably shrink 5 to 15 percent.*

"UWF at the same time wants to ensure itself an exclusive student body by viciously discouraging student enrollment in the sophomore year by individuals transferring from community colleges or even other universities.

"The total number of college–age students meanwhile is also falling drastically.

"Even the interim state education chancellor has publicly acknowledged that the demand for expanded community colleges exists while the growth needs of universities have already been sufficiently met.

"Florida has room for 105,000 full–time junior college students and needs classrooms for 125,000 full–time students.

"So how can anyone really justify putting the vested interests of industrial profiteers and power–seeking administrators before the interests of tax–paying consumers and needy families?

"I propose then a new and more informative debate of university expansion which centers on the preferred goals of increased educational quality based not on an exclusive student body but on superior teaching skills, equal access to educational opportunity for all community citizens based on high school and civic achievement and not on irrelevant admissions tests, and finally university responsiveness based on student needs and wants and not on vested commercial and political interests!"

Administrative control?

"His Reverence UWF Pres. **Robinson**, *in his Jan. 12 letter, graciously conceded he would 'gladly give space to a rebuttal'—presuming, apparently,* **he** *controls* **Voyager** *editorial policy.*

"Last quarter UWF Collections Mgr. **Phil Waltrip**, *using the pretext of my 'nonstudent status' for the last few weeks of the term, when I temporarily withdrew, pressured editor* **Bill Fielding** *into censoring my submissions.*

"UWF's administration also banned from off–campus broadcast, last quarter, a videotaped educational forum, **'Students at UWF: Are They Pawns in a Game of Repressive Tolerance?'**

"Professor **Erskine S. Dottin** *moderated campus–related discussion among five panelists, including myself and SGA executive officers.*

"Later notified of the forum taping, Fielding apparently decided against post–news coverage of the dia-

logue.

"In his Jan. 19 letter, Robinson generously granted that 'some(rebuttal comments)may be published' in the Voyager. So here's a reply concerning UWF academic advising:

"UWF's catalog, which Dean Lucius F. Ellsworth boasts 'is not a contract' reads: 'The counselor has the authority to plan a program for a student in excess of the minimums(degree requirements)listed.'

"Assigned and unsolicited counselors hold the exorbitant discretion to keep student graduations hostage by forcing them to enroll—at an unnecessary waste of time, effort and money—for more courses than minimally required by specific departments or the university itself.

"Economics instructor Janet S Miller has said that bypassing academic advisors in course scheduling makes 'a farce' of the counseling process—hard doing since the system was farcical from its inception.

"In effect, so–called counselors can prolong student graduations, indefinitely and at whim, despite the financial hardship or emotional anxiety caused students in the process.

"Obligatory academic advising should be outlawed. Counseling should be a freely voluntary, not a compulsory process.

"UWF students, Robinson writes, 'expect their mentors...to be available for counseling about academic matters.

"Unfortunately, counselors are not just 'available.'

"They're imposed on students, who unwilling to accept course dictation, are academically coerced by the threat of denied graduation.

"What's worse, most UWF counselors delude themselves into believing doctoral degrees qualify them to

lend unsolicited and 'paternalistic' advice to students on everything from personal problems to private plans.

"But it's highly doubtful students attend UWF seeking surrogate parents."

9 February 1981

§

An anonymous(**"Name Withheld"**)but sympathetic respondent wrote this **Voyager** letter–to–the–editor:

"It seems Joseph Covino, Jr. has become an issue. Although one student should not monopolize the editorial pages, it may be that he is the 'only speaker in town.' A majority of persons are apathetic in today's world so credit must be given for student concern.

*"I do agree with Mr. Covino on one issue. The Feb. 9th issue on **'Administrative Control'** struck home at the ball park. Several of my friends expressed the realism of his statements. Academic counseling should have major changes at this University. There should be both 1)general counselors who agree with the catalog or official requirements and 2)academic advisors who look at individual cases. Students should be allowed to see their choice.*

"It is a waste of taxpayer $ to require individual advisor signatures. If one follows his catalog program he knows what he needs. We are not children(or are we?). Some people like to feel they are needed—and it is nice, but that is not why we are here.

"I have had advisors of the same major give two different requirements. Upon seeing the department chairperson, the truth was revealed. Who is one to

trust if he/she can not trust his/her own advisor?

"It would be nice if advisors were more career conscious with respect to students. This is often impractical, because 'tell it like it is' doesn't hold much truth if one has never 'done it like it's done.' It is ironic that certain instructors want to tell you what it is like in the business world, when they, in fact, have never worked in the business world. If one has sales experience of three years and the advisor has sales experience of zero years, who should be telling whom about sales? What would be logical? One thing is true—we can not be all things to all people. When you don't know something, keep quiet or admit it. Don't pretend by 'storytelling.' Storytells are nice, but that is not why we are here.

"It might be helpful to think of the process as a 'joke'—it is fun. We do know that seriousness of the matter."

§

Housing explains policy positions

"In a wide–ranging 2–1/2–hour interview last Jan. 22 UWF Housing Director Bill Hudnall said his office does not always formally notify students whom it intends to evict from campus dorms.

*"Why **should** we give notice?" Hudnall asked. He qualified himself by saying that, in most eviction cases, a 48–hour notice is issued to the student by mail, phone, or through a resident assistant(RA).*

"When a student's housing contract is terminated and the vacated space reassigned to another student, Hudnall stated, UWF Housing has "no obligation" to inform the evicted tenant of its action.

"Over last Christmas break, for example, UWF

Housing evicted student Yonna Floyd from campus residence halls.

"During Floyd's absence, UWF Housing directed UWF custodian, David Gant, to remove Floyd's personal property from her room and place it in storage.

"Although Hudnall disclaimed first–hand involvement in Floyd's case, he considered it a favor that his office would store instead of discard Floyd's belongings.

"No reason for the eviction was given. And Floyd could not be reached either by mail or phone for comment.

"Hudnall questioned the use of the term "eviction" to describe a situation where a UWF student loses shelter space in which to live and occupy with possessions.

"For the 1979–80 fiscal year UWF Housing made $689 on 'new' dorms and 'something like' $2000 on 'old' dorms in late rent fee 'income.'

"To induce timely rent payment, Hudnall commented, 'you have got to have some penalty.' Private residents, for instance, are charged a $10 fee each month their rent is paid late.

"Hudnall answered the question of whether the late rent fees imposed are excessive by stating students are 'obligated to pay.'

"'It is not that they deliberately evade payment. Some do. But that's not my underlying assumption,' Hudnall responded.

"Asked, further, if UWF Housing considered a student's financial circumstances in making exceptions to rent payment deadlines Hudnall said, 'No, not generally speaking.'

"He added, however, that 'we are not going to evict students on the basis of late rent.'

"In some cases, UWF itself perpetuates a campus resident's outstanding university debt. Consider this scenario:

"A private dorm resident pays her current monthly rent on time but owes UWF a $10 late rent fee charged for a previous month.

"The student submits to the UWF cashier a check or money order, clearly designating on the payment instrument itself, that the money is to be applied toward the tenant's monthly rent bill.

*"UWF's cashier, as a debt collection practice, automatically subtracts the formerly owed $10 late rent fee from the student's **intended** current rent payment.*

"The cashier, in effect, renders the student's current payment insufficient to cover the latest monthly rent bill.

"After causing the student to pay her current monthly rent late, the cashier charges yet another $10 late rent fee for the rent payment deadline just missed.

"'I do not know by what authority it is done,' Hudnall said. 'The(cashier)procedure is to dispense with past indebtedness. It is an official policy.'

"UWF Controller Charles E. Clark wrote that it is UWF policy 'to apply any payment made by any student, first to account balances owed, and second, to accounts which are current. This policy is consistently applied to all students.'

"UWF's housing office bills students on the 15th of each month for a private room monthly rental period that starts on the 17th of each month.

"In a Nov. 4, 1980 memo, UWF Housing Director Hudnall wrote that 'a two day(payment)grace period(between the 15th and 17th of each month)does not apply.'

"Examination of one private dorm resident's rent

receipt showed that her monthly rent payment was late by two days but that UWF's cashier did not assess her housing account with a $10 late fee.

"UWF's housing office now requires dorm residents to notify it of anticipated housing contract cancellations, to avoid the $50 contract cancellation fee, a full **five** *days* **before** *students can officially withdraw from UWF with an automatic 'W' grade.*

"To illustrate: the UWF housing Winter Quarter 1981 contract cancellation deadline for students not returning Spring Quarter 1981 is Feb. 15.

"The last day students can withdraw from a course or the university with automatic 'W' grades for Winter Quarter 1981 is Feb. 20.

"As a result, students unable to determine their mid–term grades before Feb. 15 and who wait after that date to withdraw from UWF are forced to pay the $50 contract cancellation fee.

"When writing the latest UWF housing contracts, Hudnall admitted, 'we did not take into consideration the withdrawal date.'

"'It is something we did not consider. I do not think anybody even thought about it," Hudnall stated.

"Additionally, UWF's housing office allows some but not all students to live in campus housing as non–students without, as required by UWF housing contracts, prior permission from the housing director.

"'We know people get away with illegalities. All we can do is maintain a monitoring system when a problem arises,' Hudnall said.

"A student enrolled for only five credit hours who drops the course must automatically withdraw from UWF, even if the student is preregistered for classes the next quarter."

§

Karen Schulte, Voyager Copy Editor, wrote in support of free speech and free expression at UWF in her editorial dated Monday, 23 February 1981

Apathy reigns at UWF—it's time for a change

"Apathy. Websters dictionary defines it as 'lack of emotion, lack of interest, indifference.'

"That seems to be the most applicable term to describe about **90** percent of the student population at UWF. Most of you are about as active as bumps on a log. You let life slide right past you. The only time you change from your listless routine is when you notice other people doing something you do not like. Then you sluggishly drag yourself out of your hum drum rut long enough to criticize your more active peers.

"During the week that SG was involved in the controversy over the SAE beach party, you wrote letters to the **Voyager** and complained about SG activity. How many of you who wrote have ever taken notice of SG when things are going along without a hitch? How many of you who wrote were(or are)a part of SG? You signed your letters with such euphemisms as 'concerned students.' If you were really so concerned, you would be members of SG. If not members, then you would have run for an office.

"You have no right to complain about the actions of others when you are not doing anything to help or change matters any.

"The latest issue to ruffle your feathers is several letters and articles written by **Joe Covino**.

"You complain that we give too much space to him. If more of you would write to us, our pages would not have to be filled with **Covinoisms**.

"Why is it that you can not stand to see somebody do something that you are not doing also? Perhaps you are not capable of involvement or perhaps you are just envious of others' involvement.

"True, **Covino** does get a lot of space in the **Voyager** and maybe you think some of the things he writes are off–the–wall, but at least he cares about something enough to write. For this he should be commended, not condemned.

"All it would take is a few moments out of your 'busy' schedule(which include a favorite past–time: sitting in the Rat)to write us a letter and tell us what is on your mind. Jot us a note. Tell us what you would like to see covered by our staff. Take an active, not passive part in the workings of your school. You have a voice, use it for more than just complaining about what others are doing. Let your opinions be known. They are just as important as anyone else's."

§

Four–year expansion questioned

"UWF Pres. James A. Robinson is propagandizing again about the supposed merits of expanding UWF to a four–year university.

"In his Feb. 23 **Voyager** letter, ineptly trying to muster support for UWF expansion, Robinson deceptively misrepresented realities of college enrollments and social change.

"UWF planning director Dr. Pat Howe, Robinson inferred, projects 'growing' Florida college enrollments into the 1990s.

"Last April 1980, though, Dr. Howe contradicted

Robinson's current wishful thinking while discuss-ing UWF's static enrollment with fish–wrapper **Pensacola News–Journal** *staff writer* **Phylliss Sidebotham**:

"'All the baddies that they could have dreamed up have come true. They're here now: **declining** *college enrollment, inflation—you name it,' Howe herself said.*

"UWF's Fall 1980 enrollment of 5564 students, Robinson proclaimed, 'was its largest ever'—hardly anything worth bragging about.

"When Dr. Howe whined of falling college enroll-ment, about this time last year, even then only slightly more than 5000 students attended UWF.

"Despite contrary evidence, Robinson still claims college enrollments haven't peaked.

"The tremendous demand for expanding the state university system during the last 20 years, says in-terim education chancellor **Dr. George Bedell**, *has definitely tapered off.*

"Granted, colleges and universities nationwide en-rolled in 1980 a record student number: 11.7 million, up 130,000 from 1979.

"'College enrollment, however, appears to be near-ing its peak,' says the **U.S. Dept. of Education's National Center for Education Statistics**, *which projects small decreases after 1981 that will last the rest of the 1980s.*

"During the next 20 years, predicts the **Carnegie Council on Policy Studies in Higher Education**, *college enrollment nationally will probably shrink 5–15 percent.*

"Robinson qualifies his faulty optimism by assum-ing 'stability' in factors like tuition and 'availability of financial aid.'

"Budget–cutting champion Pres. Ronald Reagan

proposes that our government stop paying all interest on Guaranteed Student Loans while students attend college.

"Students would be charged 9 percent interest from the start and could borrow no more than the government decided they needed.

"Parents borrowing money under a new GSL program version would pay market rates—about 18 percent—instead of 9 percent now.

"Even low–income students would be expected to raise $750 in 'self–help' before getting a Basic Educational Opportunity Grant.

"What's worse, Reagan wants to eliminate entirely Social Security payments to students under age 22 who, when a parent dies, receive monthly benefits if they attend school full–time.

"UWF's financial aid office, admits staffer Sarah Fortino, acts as a 'screening' agency for banks or other lending institutions that finance government–insured loans.

"Instead of helping needy students as much as possible, as any public agency should, UWF's financial aid office judges which students are worthy to receive student loans by deciding for lending firms which applicants are 'good credit risks.'

"Robinson, further, indirectly blames UWF's stagnant enrollment on competition from other regional schools like Alabama's **Troy State University** *Pensacola branch.*

"Even if Troy State vanished from Pensacola, and since because of their work situations most Troy State students cannot meet the class scheduling requirements of UWF, any net gain to UWF would be negligible.

"Next, as a sly pretext for pushing UWF expansion,

Robinson masquerades as a vanguard of increased black and female university enrollments—what he labels 'important social changes.'

"Robinson conveniently forgets to mention that the state university faculty union recently charged sex discrimination against women in the state university system at UWF and eight other universities.

"The union charged the state university system discriminates against women in hiring, promotion, salary assignment, tenure and termination practices.

"Robinson conveniently omits mention of the current threat by the **U.S. Department of Education** *to cut off millions of dollars in student loans, research grants, basic grants and any* **Housing and Urban Development Department** *building programs to state universities unless Florida fully integrates its colleges.*

"Despite a 1978 integration plan to reduce the disparity of entrance rates for black and white high school graduates, that gap has actually grown since the scheme's introduction, reports U.S. assistant secretary of Education for civil rights **Cynthia G. Brown**.

"In the 1977–78 academic year, 9.9 percent fewer blacks than whites entered Florida colleges; in 1978–79 the difference rose to 15.5 percent. As 1979 began, only 5.5 percent of Florida college entrants were black, while 19.6 percent of Florida's high school graduates were black.

"Robinson expressed his true feelings about bettering equal educational access and opportunity for poor colored folk when he wrote the now–defunct **Santa Rosa Free Press:** *'I do not take the position that every high school graduate should go to college...'"*

*"***Pensacola Junior College Adult Education head Dr. June Hall** *summarizes a basic problem*

of UWF expansion proposals—bigoted exclusivism—which misleading and token statistics cannot disguise:

"'When speaking about excellency most times blacks are excluded even though there are excellent black students,' *she says.*

"UWF's plan to enroll the 'top' students, Hall warns, would turn PJC and UWF into 'two distinct segregated institutions—PJC being predominantly black or disadvantaged and UWF being predominantly white. We don't need this in this community.'

"Robinson, conveniently overlooking UWF's failed 1967 goal of enrolling 13,000 students, fully realizes that enrollment projections are overzealous distortions of enrollment actualities.

"He knows, too, that an elitist university offers not community education but is a pretentious sham.

"Sooner or later, Robinson must come out of hiding to address real issues, for his is the 'irrelevant text' our community needs to ignore."

§

Admission rules called discriminatory

"Certain bureaucratic or political connivers are propagating the viciously-conceived myth that junior colleges specialize in adult, remedial or vocational education to undermine the academic curriculum at **Pensacola Junior College(PJC).**

"The design behind their wishful thinking: solve UWF's 'image problem' nationally by attracting 'brighter,' younger and full-time students committed to four-year curriculums to UWF.

*"Concern for improving educational quality, pro-
viding equal educational opportunity for all citizens
or making the university more flexible and responsive
to student needs and wants is nonexistent.*

*"Students—being baited as a valuable Northwest
Florida resource—are being used as pawns in a collusive scheme involving a select clique of businessmen,
educrats and politicians seeking to either line their
pockets or amass greater administrative–political
power by luring new industry to Florida.*

*"Former **Gov. LeRoy Collins** has courageously
warned that **Gov. Bob Graham**'s six–member cabi-
net—sitting as **Florida's Board of Education**—
is 'comprised, of course, of people interested in other
things(besides education). It is a system that is wrong
and a system that ought to be changed.'*

*"Racist profiteers and administrative–political
power–mongers are tripping over themselves trying
to preserve their vested interests in UWF's expansion
plans.*

*"UWF's expansion reeks of discrimination against
low–income and minority students as the university
seeks tax–costly legislative appropriations to compensate itself for over–staffing and under–using its inferi-
or faculty when it reached only one–third of last year's
projected enrollment.*

*"Already **Florida's Board of Regents(BOR)**has
adopted tough new minimum entrance standards for
freshmen at the five state universities with lower–level
programs. The same is in store for UWF freshmen if
the university expands.*

*"The entrance examinations used to deny so–called
'marginal' students educational opportunity—college
admission scores having little or no correlation with
college performance—are elitist, inaccurate and in-*

valid. Yet the tests excessively influence students' educational and working careers.

"Because of falling student enrollment and declining numbers of college–age students, UWF wants to add lower classmen by draining students and funds from community colleges, private schools and even rival four–year universities.

"As UWF duplicates PJC's services, both university tuition and state taxes will rise.

"Students performing badly under the high–pressure, one–shot situation of irrelevant admission tests and those having the least ability to pay exorbitant tuition fees will be the ultimate victims of clannish, big–money designs by choice, greedy interests to further enslave our low–income population into a suppressed, ignorant class."

§

UWF–FSU merger opposition a 'vile conspiracy'

"Seeing **UWF President James Robinson***, establishment student government lackeys and other institutional vanguards aimlessly scurrying about in opposition to* **Florida's Higher Education Act** *offers liberal justice–seekers everywhere pleasant amusement.*

*"Robinson babbles about the alleged 'submergence of UWF into FSU' as threatening UWF's so–called 'autonomy,' absurdly admonishing UWF's alumni to 'prepare(themselves)to defend the autonomy and independence of(their)***alma mater.***'*

"UWF SGA President Ron VanHorn, lamenting a possible FSU–UWF merger, propagandizes students with naive notions of UWF's supposedly concerned and interested administration, which because of its

close proximity effectively communicates and best serves student needs.

"Robinson, obviously, drools at possibly being chosen from five finalists as the State University System's succeeding chancellor—an annual $65,500 position.

*"But **Florida's Board of Regents(BOR)**has postponed selecting the new chancellor until after the state legislature's June adjournment.*

"Reason: a Florida House panel recently began drafting legislation to abolish the BOR and reorganize the state's university system, including a proposal to altogether eliminate the chancellor position.

"Being an UWF alumnus in economics and criminal justice this writer asks students this question: whose 'autonomy' is really threatened—that of the larger university community or that of UWF's tottering administration?

*"The **United Faculty of Florida** urges **Gov. Bob Graham** to sign the education bill, obviously, because an $8.7 million appropriation for faculty pay raises is included in the bill.*

"Graham recently returned from his industry recruiting jaunt to Chicago, Milwaukee and New York—noting West Florida's vast resource potential of labor pool—promising his administration 'will do everything we can' to help West Florida realize its industry potential.

*"Here's the connection: former BOR member **E.W. Hopkins**, who advocated the UWF–PJC merger last year, urged 'all of West Florida to wake up...and find a system of supporting community colleges under' the university's leadership.*

"His reasoning: 'If we ever begin to get industry, it will follow a strong demonstration that our community is united and that our educational system is com-

parable to the rest of the state.'

"Students beware. A clique of fat cat Florida big-wigs are maneuvering to serve their own selfish ends while simultaneously relegating Florida's community colleges to forced specialties in adult or vocational education—excluding academic programs.

"When UWF's Robinson suggests expanding UWF to a four–year school, he doesn't talk of improving instructional quality or making his administration more responsive to student needs.

"The FSU–UWF merger opposition argument is a frail shield. A vile conspiracy is afoot, led by an alliance of frustrated businessmen and bureaucrats attempting to create or keep political power positions. They want to defeat the education bill that would curb BOR's excess authority by establishing advisory boards of trustees at each Florida university and making those schools more accountable and responsive to their student clienteles' needs.

"Gullible students fooled by the two–faced 'autonomy' rhetoric who oppose the bill will inadvertently help underpin the self–serving designs of administrative power–mongers and be this controversy's unfortunate losers."

§

NEW STUDENTS BE FOREWARNED!

"If any hindrance to your graduation exists at all—no matter how remote or obscure—UWF officials will do their utmost to deliberately frustrate you with it.

"UWF compels undergraduates, for instance, to pass two equally absurd standardized tests before UWF generously awards them their earned and bought degrees.

"The Test of Basic Math Skills(TBMS)and the Test

of Standard Written English(TSWE)are the so–called 'exit exams' required for graduation.

"Graduation–seekers who perform badly on standardized tests are forced to waste time, effort and money on UWF classes MAT 3002(Elements of Mathematics)and ENC 3453(Writing for Non–Majors) if they wish to substitute courses for the requisite tests.

"The main question concerning these ridiculous tests is not their supposed 'minimum passing requirement' or their six–time–try opportunity.

"Activist–minded education students must challenge these foolish tests on plainly simple grounds: rationale, relevance and validity.

"As a means of improving students' basic math and English skills, such asinine tests are clearly irrational, irrelevant and invalid.

"Cunningly used as just one of many ways to shore up UWF's stagnant student headcount and sustain its share of federal and state education funds, however, such inane tests are vintage but subtle UWF deceit.

"While UWF unjustly meddles in educational responsibilities better handled by pre–college schools, meanwhile, university students suffer the effects of delayed if not impeded graduations.

*"Some time ago, the **Florida Higher Education Committee**, saying state universities should get out of the business of teaching students to read and write, voted to eliminate university–level remedial education programs by 1985.*

*"'We are spending $145 million for remedial programs at the post–secondary level that could be better spent to improve the quality of education in grades kindergarten through high school,' **Rep. Bill Conway(D. Holly Hill)**told the committee.*

"Senseless remedial testing for university under-

171

grads, which is totally unrelated to their prospects for academic success, simply wastes taxpayers' money.

*"**Rep. Carrie Meeks(D. Miami)**, a teacher, has said there are students who are absolute geniuses at math or physics, but who are poor in composition.*

"Florida, she asserts, is obliged to provide an education for older adults, including the housewife who returns to the classroom after 10 years in the kitchen.

"'We must not abandon people with the aptitude for college that might lack the basic skills,' she adds. 'Even Harvard has a remedial program.'

"If students of the same graduation class would only unite to organize an 'exit exam' boycott, these stupid tests could be eradicated altogether."

§

Financial aid reliability questioned

*"UWF financial aid director C.R. Bennett is undoubtedly a **master of misinformation**.*

*"In just two brief **Voyager** interviews, Bennett has tried to hoodwink students into believing that proposed budget cuts in federal financial aid programs will have 'minimal' or 'negligible' effect on potential aid recipients.*

*"With doubletalk calculated to minimize the potentially disastrous results of Pres. Reagan's proposed education cutbacks, Bennett displays his greatest skill and favorite pastime—the **misleading statement**.*

*"Mr. Bennett boasts, for instance, that the guaranteed loan program 'will be tightened and **should** be tightened.'*

"Translation: fewer students, because of Reagan's plans to chop student aid programs down to roughly

their 1977 levels, will not be eligible to get aid they **need** *and* **deserve**.

"For a public servant who should be genuinely concerned with providing the maximum amount of financial assistance to the greatest number of needy students possible, Bennett takes a bizarre position.

"Additionally, Bennett demonstrates another area of personal expertise—the **false assumption***.*

"'I don't think it's fair for the taxpayers to be paying the interest on a student's loan because that student's parents chose not to cash some money certificates,' Bennett proclaims.

"Mr. Bennett's proficiency in making faulty and erroneous assumptions is renowned. But the facts are:

"Until 1978, students whose family income exceeded $25,000 could not get interest subsidies on nine(9) percent guaranteed student loans.

*"But the Carter administration scrapped the income cap entirely after then–***Sen. Jacob Javits, R–N.Y.,*** revealed Census Bureau evidence proving that only a small percentage of students came from families—of the 'money certificates'—earning more than $40,000.*

"Reagan now wants to eliminate the six–month repayment grace period following graduation by charging students nine(9)percent from the start of their loan award period.

"Mr. Bennett's predictably compassionate appraisal of that proposition: 'So being negatively impacted is one thing—being able to attend school is another.'

"Still, a recent **College Board** *study found that only 31 percent of freshmen from families earning less than $15,000 yearly even applied for financial aid, compared to a 41 percent three years ago.*

"Despite any so–called 'needs analysis' test of aid eligibility, it's clear that low income minority students

will suffer the most harm from budget cutbacks that will ultimately obstruct equal access to post–secondary schools.

*"Pres. Reagan, at the same time, expects low– and middle–income students to produce $750 in so–called 'self help' before getting a Basic or Pell Grant, officially named by Congress to honor **Sen. Claiborn Pell, D–R.I.**, who wrote the program ten years ago.*

"Reagan's administration claims the $750 eligibility requirement would 'eliminate benefits to the highest income students.'

"Mr. Bennett's assessment of that scheme is equally ludicrous:

"'The change is designed to cut out upper–middle income families and this will have little, if any, negative impact on UWF students because not many of our present Basic Grant students have families who receive incomes over $25,000.'

"Finally, every American college gets annual federal allocations for direct student loans, work–study employment and supplemental grants—money which is spent at the arbitrary discretion of the campus student aid director.

"UWF's financial aid director, obviously, is more interested in finding students to 'cut out' of financial help than he is in offering the most widespread assistance possible.

"Hopefully, UWF's Student Government Association will investigate and report publicly on the dismal educational prospects for students enduring this shameful situation."

Financial aid assessment questioned

"The headline captioning UWF financial aid di-

rector *C.R. Bennett's recent* **Voyager** *column* **should** *have read: Making* **NON**–*sense.*

"*Mr. Bennett's newly gotten doctoral title, apparently, now qualifies him to be a public opinion expert and popular sentiment pollster.*

"'**Most** *Americans support President Reagan's Economic Recovery Plan,' he absurdly declares—as if he spoke for anyone for himself.*

"'**We** *applaud loudly the need,' for economic restraint and self–sacrifice, Bennett foolishly proclaims, 'until the sacrifice becomes too personal.'*

"*Is* **anyone** *irked when* **any** *administrative buffoon tries to characterize a majority national population with ridiculous generalizations?*

"*An economic slump period, needing consumer leaning remedies, is an odd time to start holding 'the erosion of traditional student and family responsibility for post–secondary education.'*

"*Translation: the Reagan administration—with an attitude Mr. Bennett likely shares—is mostly unconcerned about helping needy students, who without ample financial assistance, simply cannot afford to attend college.*

"*Despite incomplete and unrepresentative opinion polls, considerable opposition to Reagan's education cutback scheme exists. Some examples:*

"**The Coalition of Independent College and University Students** *and the* **U.S. Student Association** *organized the lobbying effort.*

"•**Sen. Mark Andrews, R–N.D.**, *recently revealed how the Reagan administration is trying to keep ranch and farm children from getting guaranteed student loans because of the land their parents own.*

"*The average North Dakota farmer, Andrews reports, has an $89,000 farm equity, but earns only*

$2700 yearly from the equity.

"Additionally, the Reagan administration wants to make the income cutoff for farm families under the basic educational opportunity grant program $21,000 instead of the previously set $25,000.

*"•**Florida Sen. Clark Maxwell, Jr., R–Melbourne**, recently warned how Reagan's education cuts would virtually shut off some $6 million in federal school aid going to Florida school districts educating children of federal employees.*

"Reagan budgeteers would restrict eligibility for federal impact aid to districts where 20 percent or more of the children come from federally employed families—a policy Maxwell reports would penalize countywide Florida districts.

*"•Equal access to post–secondary schools for minorities will likewise buckle under Reaganite cuts, reports **Florida University System Chancellor Barbara Newell**.*

*"UWF's financial aid director, meantime, propagandizes us on the availability of grant, loan and work moneys for '**all** with **documented** need' and that 'all applications are offered the **fullest consideration** for merit and need–based dollars.'*

*"Actually, since federal allocations for direct student loans, work–study employment and supplemental grants are spent at the arbitrary discretion of the financial aid director—and **not** on the basis of objective aid formulas—'**need**' has little if any bearing on the distribution of these funds.*

*"In practice, the financial aid director—for whatever petty or childish personal excuse—can discriminate against **any** financial aid application—**regardless** of need.*

"To investigate and expose the fraudulent practices

of UWF's financial aid office, our Student Government Association **must** *both openly and secretly monitor its activities, soliciting documented statements from financial aid applicants and recipients, cultivating civic–minded whistleblowers working inside the office.*

"Findings should then be compiled and publicly reported in the Voyager.

"Well, SG? Do you have the backbone for this **kind** *of worthwhile work?"*

Monday, 18 May 1981

§

Enrollment may be discouraged

"UWF 'will discourage enrollment in the sophomore year to avoid drawing students from a community college or another university.

"That's exactly how **Pensacola News–Journal** *writer* **Jo Ann Gordon** *quoted an unnamed UWF 'official' in a recent news report describing the university's proposed four–year academic curriculum.*

"UWF's planned admission requirements and four–year program, reported Gordon, are meant to attract high school seniors who would otherwise attend a four–year school and encourage admission at the freshman or junior year.

"Florida education officials, meanwhile, are scrambling to boost state schools into America's 'top quartile'—or upper 25 percent—during the next five years.

"America's 'top quartile' refers to the 12 top–ranked states in evaluations of school progress devised by the **National Education Association***.*

"Apparently, UWF's chief strategy to entice Florida's

so–called 'brighter' students and thereby raise its academic standing involves tougher admission requirements.

"Stiffer entrance requirements, in turn, means a heavier emphasis on standardized admission tests. Freshmen applicants at UWF, for instance, must score at or above the 50th percentile on national norms established by the **American College Test** *or* **Scholastic Aptitude Test***.*

"At the same time, reports **Associated Press writer Ken Klein***, executives of the firms that distribute the tests caution against using college entrance exam scores to compare quality of schools because only a fraction of the student population takes the tests.*

"Consumer advocate **Ralph Nader***, additionally, reports there is little or no correlation between college admission test scores and college academic performance.*

"Nader faults entrance exams for measuring 'little more than the ability of students in a one–shot, high pressure situation to match words and do arithmetic.'

"Such tests, Nader says, fail to assess more important skills needed for success in school and later life. Exams 'do not measure stamina, creativity, dedication, leadership and all the other human qualities which have marked the progress of civilization.'

"While there's only one opportunity to take the tests, Nader says they have an **'overpowering influence'** *on students' academic and working careers.*

"High school grades are better indicators than test scores of how well students will do in college, Nader asserts. **'You cannot determine people's careers on the basis of how they happen to do in three hours,'** *he adds.*

"Tests that 'don't measure judgment, wisdom, experience, creativity, stamina, determination— the actual characteristics that make for progress in human history' cannot accurately predict any student's first–year college grades, Nader warns.

"Florida Gov. Bob Graham's $20.3 billion recommended 1981–83 budget allots $778,000 in 1983 for a lower–division program at UWF for 300 students—to meet what one Florida legislator calls an undetermined need.

"Because UWF seeks to cultivate a select and exclusive student body, the result may be that some students who perform badly on standardized tests may be denied admission or will be forced to lower career sights in favor of less fulfilling employment.

"While UWF would deny that enrolling a choice group of 'cream of the crop' students excludes other capable and deserving students from educational opportunity, Ralph Nader prefers that 'schools admit they are elitist and educate the elite and have it out in the open.'

Monday, 8 June 1981

§

SGA wastes valuable time

*"UWF's SGA **sometimes** misdirects well–intentioned efforts by wasting valuable time on **relatively** unimportant matters.*

*"Constitutional procedure and SGA Pres. **Ron VanHorn**'s budget and appointment practices, prominent SGA concerns, certainly must never be minimized or overlooked.*

*"But **Ron VanHorn** and Student Advocate **Linda***

179

Hamel—*I can personally attest—are both first–rate, help–minded public servants.*

"For their diligent service and genuine concern for students, they each deserve much more student appreciation and gratitude than they currently get.

"Neither of them, I'm confident, would wittingly shirk their official duties or breach their public trust by exploiting their positions for self–serving ends.

*"Unlike most inflexible and unresponsive UWF officials, **Ron VanHorn** especially is open–minded and receptive enough to approach unique individuals, isolated problems and separate circumstances without childish prejudgment or presumption.*

"Students having problems at UWF are well–advised to seek the assistance of responsible student representatives who remain truly sensitive to student needs and wants.

"Real decision– and policy–making authority affecting student interests naturally resides with a few, select UWF officials who stay mostly indifferent to student desires.

"UWF officialdom is largely held unaccountable for university practices and policies which harm untold numbers of students suffering the dire consequences of misused and abused authority.

*"While SG expends precious time and energy investigating real or imagined wrongs supposedly committed within its own ranks, dubious **university** actions go unchallenged, unchecked and uncorrected.*

*"As SG preoccupies itself with extensive probes into mostly unfounded or unproved corruption among its peers, **university**–instigated injustice and oppression against students intensify until they become institutionalized.*

"When personality conflicts, ego trips and petty

jealousies predominate SGA business, meanwhile, the human casualties of students enduring university maltreatment burgeon.

"Unnecessary and superfluous internal squabbling only distracts SG from its first obligation to safeguard and promote student interests.

"The right of SG to police itself and maintain high ethical standards is unquestioned. If definite and conclusive misdeeds arise, SG must act quickly to rectify them.

*"SG must likewise monitor **university** performance with equal vigilance. Prolonged and needless SG bickering, internally, only perpetuates **dis**organization.*

*"If useless internal disputes cause SG to neglect protection of student interests—and **university** malpractice escapes reform—students themselves are indeed **dis**serviced.*

*"The efficacy of any SG inquiry certainly cannot be second–guessed here. But SG only silently sanctions and legitimizes those questionable **university** behaviors that, for whatever reason, go unprotested and unreproved.*

"For without doubt, preserving student expectations and achieving student aspirations must together, above all else, become SG's chief goal and highest priority.

"Realizing that university abuse which hurts just one person can potentially damage everyone is the first stage toward distinguishing between importance and trivia."

§

The pros of UWF expansion plan rejection

"Enormous praise belongs to state lawmakers for their wise and commendable decision to reject expansion of UWF to a four–year school.

"Florida legislators struck down hard UWF's failed attempt to become an elite school with an exclusive and segregated student body.

"Immediate benefits to our community which result because of the judicious and well–advised action our laudable state legislature took include:

"•Preserving Pensacola Junior College's superior academic curriculum. The college's students were not simply shifted to UWF and its chief task was not purposefully relegated to adult, remedial and vocational schooling.

"•Retaining equal access to higher education in our community. All high school graduates—especially those UWF officials high–handedly label "marginal" or audaciously deem undeserving of higher education—will not be denied at least a two–year college education for doing badly on standardized university admissions tests.

"•Accumulated tax dollar savings for citizens. Duplicated community educational services, higher consumer costs due to increased university salaries and added administrative support personnel, and over–inflated university tuition fees were effectively rebuffed.

"•High quality education re–confirmed. The preferred values of superior teaching and research performance were re–emphasized over using UWF to advance the moneyed concerns of economic developers and prestige–seeking sports promoters.

*"•Re–affirming the **primary** mission of higher learning institutions: education and enlightenment. Pocket–lining connivings by a few profiteers, educrats*

and politicians to use UWF as a supplier for over–specialized laborers for new Florida–locating industries flopped.

"The need for UWF expansion just wasn't there. The tremendous demand for expanding the state university system, interim education chancellor Dr. George Bedell has said, has definitely tapered off.

"If UWF had been allowed to admit college freshmen based on performance and academically irrelevant and culturally biased entrance exams, before high school and civic achievement, equal educational opportunity for low–income and low–mobility minority students would have disappeared.

"This writer, for one, is absolutely pleased and utterly delighted that state lawmakers ultimately put the needs of tax–paying consumers and needy families before vested commercial and political interests.

*"There is, after all, **some** justice left in the world"*

§

Tenants, know your legal rights

"While student residents simmer in the sweltering summer heat engulfing poorly cooled UWF dormitories, rent paying tenants anywhere locally can ask themselves: how can landlords be persuaded to improve sick living conditions?

"Before answering that question—and since simple ignorance can be a tenant's worst enemy—let's first review some basic facts:

"A rental lease is a binding legal agreement between a landlord and a tenant, enforceable through the courts, that defines the respective rights and obligations of both contracting parties regarding the ten-

ancy.

"Oftentimes, many leases contain numerous ob-noxious or even illegal clauses—the most repugnant provisos requiring that a tenant waive existing legal rights and remedies concerning occupancy.

"Although some jurisdictions prohibit the waiver by a lease of certain rights, your signature on the lease agreement is usually sufficient evidence that you read the lease and consented to its terms and conditions.

"But don't let any contract waiving landlord fool or intimidate you with huffy claims that all lease provi-sions are absolutely binding. Because they're not.

"As a renter, you have the perfectly legitimate option to negotiate either the amendment or the total and complete exclusion of any obnoxious lease stipulation that restricts your tenant rights.

*"If you **don't** exercise your right to negotiate your rental lease agreement, you risk the pitfall of some unscrupulous landlord later using an obnoxious or il-legal clause as a trumped up excuse to evict you.*

*"Most importantly, remember: just because you sign a lease agreement does **not** mean that you cannot later contest obnoxious or illegal clauses which state courts may declare void and unenforceable.*

"Assuming that as part of your rental agreement, your landlord is responsible for providing utility ser-vices, a prime example of an obnoxious clause is any provision which tries to limit a landlord's liability for acts that damage a tenant's person or property.

"UWF student housing contracts, for instance, have several obnoxious—or "exculpatory clauses"—one of which reads:

"THE UNIVERSITY IS NOT FINANCIALLY LIABLE FOR FAILURE OF UTILITIES OR MECHANICAL EQUIPMENT."

"When a landlord wrongfully shuts off utility service, a tenant—with a lawyer's help—can seek a court order—"injunctive relief"—requiring immediate restoration of utility services.

"Landlords who refuse to comply with court ordered injunctions may be jailed or fined.

"Whether or not the state has laws granting damages for utility shutoffs, you may also be entitled to damages for the time period you were forced to live without utility service.

*"Utility shutoffs almost always mean a situation which violates your implied "warranty of habitability" guarantee—your assured right to minimum standards of decent housing and the option **not** to pay for "essential services" or decent housing which you do not receive.*

"The contractual guarantee that the landlord must provide tenants with decent, safe, sanitary and habitable housing is implied by law in every oral or written residential rent agreement made.

"It cannot be waived by private agreement, either—even if your lease specifically rejects it or fails to mention it.

"Although Florida recognizes warranty of habitability, the courts decide on a case by case basis when a defective condition proves a breach of the warranty.

"In most jurisdictions that accept the warranty, housing codes determine particular standards of decency, safety, sanitation and habitability.

"Housing codes are state or local legislative statements which mandate minimum health and safety standards for residential housing and oblige landlords to maintain rental property in compliance with those guidelines.

"All housing codes regulate room temperature, wa-

ter temperature and pressure, electrical and fire safety, workable plumbing, rodent and insect infestation and building structure.

"Specifically, a substantial housing code violation must affect a dwelling's livability or the tenant's health or safety before a warranty breach can be shown.

"As you probably expect, the failure of neglectful municipal building inspection departments to cite housing code violators, frequent extensions of repair dates and court refusals to fine or jail offending land-lords exemplify traditional housing code enforcement.

"The best way to redress your housing grievances is bringing civil suit for damages against your land-lord for violating habitability—but using local hous-ing codes to define the minimum decent housing stan-dards breached.

"A copy of a housing code violation report—which is public information available on request—is the best evidence you can have to prove habitability violations should you sue your landlord in court.

"Next time, we'll survey the usual procedure of re-porting housing code violations and other tenant rem-edies for substandard or deficient housing—including partial or nonpayment of rent and tenant organizing.

"Meanwhile, here are the addresses and phone numbers—for those of you undocile tenants who want to complain now—of state and local building inspec-tion authorities:...

"Don't just sit there reading. Start demanding your rights—**now!**"

Monday, 27 July 1981

§

Housing codes worth investigation

"Housing codes may oblige landlords in legal statute to uphold minimum standards of habitable housing but are worthless if they remain unenforced.

*"Whether broad or detailed in scope, housing codes alone cannot guarantee you the decent, liveable dwelling you deserve. Much of their **practical** application and coverage depend on **your own** willingness to **demand** code enforcement.*

"As mentioned before, housing codes are state or local laws which set minimum standards for safe, clean and comfortable habitation.

"Among other things, these legislative regulations bind your landlord to: keep your building fully repaired; sufficiently clean and light your halls; supply adequate room and water temperature control; and properly maintain your plumbing and electrical systems.

"Local housing code department inspectors— though they often won't—should check out all tenant complaints about code violation.

"Depending on the results of their examinations, inspectors may issue summonses which order landlords who violate housing codes to correct the infractions; landlords refusing compliance can be fined.

*"If designated public officials fail to enforce housing codes, tenants themselves must seek **independent** remedies for substandard or deficient housing.*

*"In other words, you must take **direct action** when your landlord deprives you of essential building services which you contracted and paid for.*

"Here's how to report housing code violations:

*"•Telephone your local building inspection department to register your complaint and **request an inspection** of your residence.*

"•Be present on the day and time of the inspector's

arrival to show the conditions needing repair, doing everything possible to help the inspector notice and record these conditions on paper.

"•Urge the inspector to carefully examine the rest of your dwelling and the common areas of your building for other code violations you may have missed.

*"•**Get a copy of the inspection report**—usually in a few days—by making a copy yourself at the inspection department or by paying to have one sent to you.*

"•If housing code violations exist, check to ensure that a copy of the inspection report is served on the landlord with an order to repair within a specified time period of around 30 to 60 days.

*"Inspection reports are public information and are available to you on request. If **errors or omissions** in the report exist, telephone the inspection department to request changes or even a new inspection.*

"Repeated phone calls to the building inspection department may be needed to push the code enforcement process. But be sure to attend any department or court hearing on your particular case to ensure that your version of the problem is properly reported and recorded.

"Remember, too, that your 'implied warranty of habitability' is also probably violated when your landlord breaks housing code rules.

"The warranty guarantees you the right to minimum standards of decent housing and that you need not pay for 'essential services' or decent housing you do not receive.

"Implied in every oral or written residential rent agreement, this contractual guarantee requires your landlord to provide you with decent, safe, sanitary and habitable housing.

"Building inspection reports citing housing code violations are usually the best evidence and proof of breaches of the warranty.

"Florida recognizes warranty of habitability—a standard usually defined by housing codes.

"If you sue your landlord in court for violating your habitability, the court considers these factors in deciding whether your landlord has breached the warranty:

"•Has any applicable housing code, building or sanitation regulation been violated?

"•Does the nature of the deficiency or defect affect a vital facility?

"•Does it potentially or actually affect safety or sanitation?

"•How long has it persisted?

"•How old is the structure?

"•How much is rent?

"•Is the tenant at all responsible for the defective condition?

"Tenants acting alone or with others can exercise other remedies useful against landlords failing to provide decent, safe, sanitary and habitable housing.

"Court action often follows when a landlord challenges the validity of the remedy used.

"But if the tenant carefully chooses the right remedy, follows the correct procedures and proper methods, few problems should occur when and if the matter reaches trial.

"Tenant remedies usually employed include repair and deduct, rent abatement and injunctive relief.

"A tenant can sue a landlord for breaching the habitability warranty or can use the warranty breach itself as a defense to a landlord's suit for eviction.

"Apart from withholding rent payments or deducting self–incurred repair expenses from the rent, ten-

ants can even organize and initiate building wide rent strikes and landlords cannot lawfully retaliate against you with eviction notice simply because you exercised these perfectly lawful rights!

*"**WARNING:** check state or local laws to find out if a particular tenant remedy exists in your locale or has been modified by recent legal changes.*

"Next time, we'll discuss in full detail these tenant remedies for substandard or defective housing.

*"A UWF flier entitled '**Off the Wall**' frequently issues 'reminders' of what students can do—aside from exercising legal rights, naturally—to alleviate housing problems.*

"Concerning roach bug infestation, for instance, the publication condescends and admonishes students for **'wasting time running around complaining.'**

"But for certain action on your insect or rodent complaint, ignore official pronouncements which discourage you from using legitimate means to redress your equally legitimate housing grievances.

"Contact the insect and rodent control division of Escambia County's Health Department..."

Monday, 3 August 1981

§

Tenants unite; power rests in consolidation

"The rule's simple: there's strength in numbers.

"Tenant associations are a sure way to get landlord action on your housing complaints—if leaders exist to form and organize them, that is.

"Unless you want the same constant housing problems facing you now to continue uncorrected, indefi-

nitely, act **collectively** *to bring* **organized** *pressure against indifferent and unresponsive landlords.*

"*Collective tenant action on housing grievances reduces the risk of landlord retaliation. The more tenants organize, the more effective their redress action will be.*

"*Begin tenant organization in your own building by just knocking on doors, posting notices and scheduling tenant meetings.*

"*But caution is warranted: if you are uncommitted or unwilling to devote much time and energy over extended time periods to tenant organizing, forget any chances of successfully influencing neglectful and irresponsible landlords who, despite hypocritical claims to the contrary, care less about your living conditions.*

"*If you successfully organize yourself, achieve positive results on your various housing complaints but make the tragic mistake of disbanding, you'll be unprepared to properly meet future difficulties when they come.*

"*For one thing's sure: an ongoing tenant association is your safest bet to get your landlord's attention and response in the future, too.*

"*A potent persuader tenant associations use to move negligent landlords is organized 'rent abatement.'*

"*Tenants need not pay full rent if their housing is uninhabitable.*

"*In states like Florida, which observe 'warranty of habitability,' tenants simply need not pay for 'essential services' they do not get.*

"*Basically, the rent abatement remedy is a claim for civil damages which tenants may:*

"*•initiate against the landlord.*

"*•use as a defense against a landlord's claim for back rent.*

"•use as a defense against eviction for nonpayment of rent for uninhabitable housing.

"Unless state law demands more specific procedures, tenants can withhold all or part of the rent due for unlivable housing.

"Finally, the courts determine the actual amount of rent reduction involved. After reviewing the defective conditions breaching the warranty, the courts decide the properness of using the rent abatement remedy.

"In any case, the remedy monetarily compensates tenants for warranty violations and, by lowering the rent level, gives landlords an economic incentive to make repairs.

"Practically, rent strike, rent withholding and rent abatement have equal effect—keeping rent money from landlords who breach your warranty of habitability.

"Rent withholding or abatement laws sometimes require protesting tenants to deposit withheld rent money into special court escrow accounts.

"Collective rent strikes are preferable and more effective remedies, however, in accomplishing limited tenant goals. Here's how they're used:

"•Decide if the defective housing conditions breach your warranty of habitability.

"•Serve your landlord written notice, using certified mail, to make repairs.

"•If repairs are not done after a reasonable opportunity and time period, withhold all or part of your next monthly rent payment.

"If you act in good faith and comply with applicable state law, no penalty exists for withholding all the rent.

"Since the court decides the final amount of rent abatement, you may only get the rent portion you withhold if you don't withhold it all.

"•*File an* **affirmative damage action** *against your landlord to initiate the rent abatement action yourself.*

"•*While seeking damages, sue affirmatively at the same time for* **'declaratory and injunctive relief,'** *asking the court to order your landlord to make repairs or cease violating housing code standards.*

"A landlord under injunction who refused to perform court ordered obligations is held in contempt of court.

"The chief advantage of getting an injunction is the court ordered **'specific performance'** *of the habitability warranty that compels your landlord to keep your premises livable.*

"Moreover, affirmative civil action in a court of regular jurisdiction permits you to seek wider damages, including retroactive rent abatement or return of rent paid over time, future rent abatement and compensating damages for personal injury or property damage.

"The drawback: litigation in a civil court of general jurisdiction is costly. But it avoids the limited, summary nature of eviction court which, if your landlords takes you there but you win, awards you damages for only the months you withhold rent. So pool your resources, too.

"And remember: to speak, peacefully assemble or petition your government for a redress of grievances are your constitutional rights. Let no one browbeat you into believing an exercise of your rights is **'radical'** *or unethical.*

"Landlords cannot lawfully harass, punish or retaliate against tenants exercising their legal rights or engaging in lawful activities.

"Florida, specifically, prohibits retaliation by landlords who would evict you, raise your rent or cut ser-

vices simply because you executed your rights.

"Landlords cannot evict you for either reporting housing code violations to enforcement agencies or tenant organizing.

"If you stay docile, you can count on your landlord to persist in abusing you.

"Now some words on eviction:

*"Landlords themselves cannot lawfully evict tenants. In nearly all states, only courts can evict tenants. For whatever reason or cause, **all** states have statutory schemes for eviction, most requiring at least minimal court involvement.*

*"All states require a landlord to give a tenant notice of intention to initiate legal proceedings for eviction **before** the landlord can even file a court complaint.*

"UWF housing contracts have an illegal clause— "The resident must vacate the residence hall within 48 hours of withdrawal, suspension, release or termination of the contract"—which stands only because it remains unchallenged in court.

"Normally, most jurisdictions require a 30–day or one–month notice for terminating a monthly tenancy...

"An improperly served eviction notice may invalidate itself, forcing the landlord to refile the complaint.

"In many states, a court that decides against you may even stay or postpone eviction if immediate eviction imposes hardship on you.

"Even if the court does not stay the eviction, state law often allows a short time period between the eviction court order and the actual move out date.

"The important point is: although your housing lease or contract may, on the surface, seem to exempt your landlord from various tenant legal protections, any obnoxious contract clause can be negotiated or fought in civil court.

"*Safeguarding and preserving your tenant rights is mostly up to you. Much more can and will be written on tenant rights.*

"*For now, here are some addresses of organizations that advocate tenant rights and provide information on the subject:…*

"*If your landlord won't deal with tenant organizers, picketing and adverse publicity are also effective but last resort remedies against unheedful landlords quick to take your money, disclaim your tenant rights but slow to provide you with the service of decent, habitable housing.*

"*So remember: even if your housing contract is expired or terminated, it's never too late to collect civil damages for violations of your tenant rights—**wherever** you decide to nest.*"

Monday, 31 August 1981

§

Legal action; not necessarily an expensive step

"*Ignore this dangerous myth: the financial cost of legal action against negligent or corrupt organizations which deliberately wrong individuals is prohibitive.*

"*Tragically, the fantasy that all lawsuits are super expensive or 'unrealistic' deters many people with justified legal claims against organizations from suing them cheaply in county court.*

"*UWF officials who perpetuate the myth, for instance, sit pretty believing that gullible students fooled by it are neatly restrained from exercising their legal rights to collect moneyed damages.*

"*Suppose the university or some organization owes*

you money but illegally refuses to pay up.

"For a mere $33 'filing fee,' you can file a 'summary claim' in county court against any organization owing you money for up to $1500.

"Here's the easy way to sue:

"•Contact the 'summary claims' division of the Escambia County Court...

"•The County Court Clerk helps you complete the forms for filing suit.

"•In court, the judge listens to both opposing sides and decides who wins. If the judgment does not favor you, only the filing fee is lost.

"•You can even ask for a jury trial, but it costs extra filing fees.

"•To serve the suit papers on the organization involved, you pay just $12 for sheriff's service or you can serve them yourself by certified mail for about $1.75.

"Even if you lose your case, you can at least send a message to the offending organization that it cannot forever continue its malpractices or mistreatments of people free of repercussion and inconvenience.

"Besides, dragging your organizational nemesis into court can alone be fun.

"The county court can give you more detailed information on filing suit and trial procedures, as well as getting your money after a favorable judgment.

"Meantime, for those readers serious about filing a summary claims lawsuit, two inexpensive books can help you prepare your case and show you how to take legal action cheaply, quickly—and without a lawyer:..."

§

No work–no money policy instituted at UWF

"University of West Florida(UWF)financial aid director and resident demigod C.R. Bennett now proclaims from on high that he commands the authority to coerce students into accepting on–campus jobs against their better judgment.

"If students refuse to kowtow to Mr. Bennett's administrative blackmail, he threatens to withhold from them certain kinds of moneyed assistance.

"Specifically, Mr. Bennett claims he can deny 'need–based' loans and supplemental grants to students who decline to accept campus–based, part–time employment.

"He expects, in effect, that the can force students to choose a particular type of financial aid—at his whimsical beck and call—in order to receive another type.

*"In practice, any school financial aid director has the extreme discretion to arbitrarily discriminate against any financial aid applicant—regardless of the student's **'need.'***

"A financial aid director can, for instance, disqualify a student from getting guaranteed student loan funds by arbitrarily refusing to 'certify' the student's loan application.

"At UWF, this action is routine.

"Mr. Bennett also claims that his latest administrative 'workfare' extortion 'has met with virtually no resistance' from students involved.

"From the start of their educations, college students are programmed over the years to be docile and voluntarily fill out and sign whatever form is put before them, or gullibly believe whatever claptrap educrats bombard them with.

"And if you believe in 'studies,' there undoubtedly exist several which prove that over–worked and over–

pressured students taking full–time class loads make poor academic grades.

"The important point is: Mr. Bennett is trying to hoodwink our community into believing he can dictate to students their otherwise free choice of alternative financial aid programs.

"If you object to this brand of high and mighty browbeating, or doubt that Mr. Bennett can lawfully bully students into being minimum wage lackeys for UWF—and want to know what Mr. Bennett **hasn't** *told you—please complain to:*

"U.S. Dept. of Education..."

Monday, 21 September 1981

§

Security deposit—an easy mark for landlord abuse

"An easy mark for landlord abuse is the security deposit—the sum of money a tenant pays the landlord to help ensure the tenant abides by the terms of the rental agreement and relevant laws.

"It also gives the landlord a hedge against any future debt the tenant is claimed to owe.

"Since the landlord holds your money, you shoulder the burden of any court action started to prove that any debt later deducted from your deposit is not really owed.

"Unfortunately, most landlords regard the security deposit not as a refundable deposit, but instead relish it as an extra part of their profit margin.

"No state law either requires or forbids tenants to pay—or landlords to collect—a security deposit as a

pre–condition of the tenancy.

"Though most landlords require a security deposit payment before you move in, any such deposit is legally open to negotiation.

"Most states broadly protect tenant rights in the collection and return of security deposits—and limit the amount of security a landlord can oblige you to pay.

"In Florida, however, no maximum security deposit is provided for. But your landlord must pay you up to five percent interest a year on your deposit...

"Take special note here: a so–called **'non–refundable'** *security deposit is an illegal obnoxious clause wherever it exists.*

"If the tenant meets all the conditions specified in the rental agreement's security clause, **any** *and* **all** *security deposits are by their very definition* **refundable***.*

"Usually a security deposit cannot lawfully be an advance, prepayment or financial penalty for particular damages.

"Your rental agreement may allow your landlord to deduct set sums of money from your security deposit for certain tenant acts—but no deductions can be made unless the acts actually occur.

"Lease agreement clauses which specify the amount of damages before the events actually occur—what contract jargon labels **'liquidated damages'***—are indeed legally suspect.*

"When a deduction charge from your security deposit does not mirror the landlord's costs, it becomes an illegal penalty and can be reduced in 'summary claims' court to the amount of damages, if any, the landlord actually proves.

"So if and when you terminate your tenancy, your landlord better be ready to pay back your deposit mi-

nus any reasonable and justifiable deductions.

"All states with security deposit safeguards require landlords to notify their tenants in writing, within a legally specified time frame, of any and all deductions from your deposit.

"In Florida, you must receive a written list of itemized deductions from the deposit which specify the nature and amount of the subtractions.

"At the same time, you must receive a check from the landlord which equals the full security deposit you paid minus deductions.

"Florida landlords have just 15 days to itemize these security deductions—and tenants have 15 more days to object to any such subtractions after the tenancy ends.

"As a result, Florida landlords have 30 days to refund tenant security deposits once the lease terminates.

"So if you fail to take your landlord to 'summary claims' court when your security deposit is illegally withheld, or when an itemized list of security deductions is not provided, you only encourage corrupt landlords to continue abusing tenant deposits.

"UWF student housing contracts carry these illegal obnoxious clauses related to security deposits—but disguised as pre–payments or fees:

"•'After an assignment has been made for the initial semester of the contract, the $50.00 pre-payment will be forfeited if the students does not accept the space assigned.'

"But non–refundable deposits are illegal.

"•'A $10.00 late fee will be charged for all payments received after the 15th of each month.'

"But pre–determined contract damages are legally suspect.

"•'If written notice of cancellation is received

and approved by the Department of Housing after the official cancellation of contract deadline but before the official opening of the residence halls for the initial semester of occupancy, a refund for all sums paid for the semester—LESS $50.00—will be made.'

"But non–refundable deposits are illegal.

"•*'If written notice of cancellation is received and approved by the Department of Housing through the Friday ending the second week of classes, ONE MONTH'S RENT PLUS $50.00 will be assessed or withheld for the semester.'*

"But non–refundable deposits are illegal.

"•*'If the request is approved after the cancellation date, the resident will be assessed $50.00 and one month's rent.'*

"But non–refundable deposits are illegal.

"•*'A $25.00 extermination of pests fee may be assessed against a resident for violation of the pet regulation,'* among other possible charges.

"But pre–determined contract damages are legally suspect.

"Since the landlord already has your money, it's your responsibility to challenge the landlord's unfair retention of all or part of your security deposit.

"In the 'summary claims' division of county court, you may question the need, reasonableness and amount of any deposit deduction, as well as the landlord's refusal to return any of your deposit.

"A landlord has a good little racket going when you're charged for phony undocumented damages, or when you're stalled off until you're frustrated enough to forfeit your just due refund.

"So here's what to do about unjustified over–charges and security deductions:

"•Pre–rental inventory. When you first move in, check your residence carefully for any existing defects and have your landlord agree to fix them.

"•About a week before moving out, give your landlord your new mailing address with instructions where to send your security deposit check.

"•If you haven't gotten your check within the month after your tenancy ends, remind your landlord to refund all or part of your money—along with an itemized accounting.

*"**IMPORTANT:** In Florida, a landlord forfeits the right to retain anything from your security deposit if an itemized accounting is not provided to you **before the legal deadline.***

"Florida law also allows you to collect more than just the amount of money being wrongfully withheld from your security deposit(attorney fees and court costs).

"If your landlord refuses to make an itemized accounting, or gobbles up your security deposit by doctoring the accounting with a bunch of trumped up expenses, follow this process:

*"•If you don't know what they are, determine the exact nature and cause of the damages claimed. You are not responsible for '**ordinary wear and tear**' of the premises.*

*"•If the landlord insists on exaggerating the damages claimed, state your intention to sue for your own '**damages**' within ten days.*

"•Don't make idle threats. Drag your landlord into county court and sue for money damages. The court costs are minimal and hiring a lawyer isn't necessary.

"If you win your lawsuit, the landlord is stuck with the court costs anyway—and justice is done.

"So go for it!"

Monday, 5 October 1981

§

Student rights to protect privacy of school records

"University students who want to protect the privacy of their school records—or what's left of it—should be informed about certain rights university officials would prefer keeping secret.

"Federal law allows students to access to their own school records on demand and limits their disclosure to outsiders. Students may also demand from the university copies of *all* their educational files.

"**The Family Rights and Privacy Act(1974)**, or the **Buckley Amendment**, named after its sponsor, former **New York Senator James L. Buckley**, gives students these protections.

"Under it, the university cannot disclose either academic or personal information to even local, state or federal government agencies, like the FBI, police, civil service or military intelligence.

"If the university violates the law with a policy or practice of releasing educational records about students without their written consent, it can be denied federal funds.

"By law, the university cannot disclose student records to other school officials, including those elsewhere in the school system or to other schools where you may seek to enroll, **unless you're notified**.

"Although it doesn't, the university must notify you of your access rights to student records each year.'

"Even former students have the right of individual access to their educational records. Medical records, *too, may be shared with any medical professional of your choice.*

"Technically, the university has 45 days to give you access to your educational files, but cannot destroy the records in the interim.

"To effectively inspect your record, however, you have the right to make notes or take photocopies of your student files. Faculty recommendations are not exempt from your right to access.

"When any part of your educational records is inac-curate or mis–leading, follow this process:

"•demand that school officials change the mis–information.

"•demand that the school place your written response to the mis–information in the record to always accompany your file.

*"•if the university refuses to comply with your just demands, complain to the nearest **U.S. Education Dept.** regional office, giving specific reference to the **'Privacy Office.'**...*

"Don't hesitate to complain about fallacious student records. Even if your individual problem is unresolved, your complaint can support reform at the university.

"And remember: university compiled student records are private facts entitled to full constitutional protection.

*"Students have a constitutional right to privacy in the personal information collected about them and can enforce their right to protect it independently in the courts—whether or not the **Buckley Amendment** applies."*

Monday, 19 October 1981

§

Tenant's right to privacy—covenant of quiet enjoyment

"It's called the covenant of quiet enjoyment.

"This implied or written rental agreement clause protects a tenant's right to privacy against unwarranted intrusions into your living unit by nosy or intimidating landlords.

"Further, it guarantees your exclusive right to possess and occupy your rental unit without wrongful intrusions by any outsider—your landlord included.

"If your landlord enters your residence lacking your authorization, the covenant is violated and a trespass is committed on your property.

"And you can sue for money damages if your landlord encroaches on your dwelling, harms any of your belongings or acts violently.

"You may even sue for the mental distress your landlord's incursion causes you.

"Generally, you may refuse your landlord admittance to your abode in non–emergency situations, especially when the landlord arrives at your door, unannounced, at odd hours.

"But if your landlord—or any landlord employee—invades your lodging lacking your permission, or without any reasonable justification, a trespass on your private property occurs.

"Your chief guide in most situations is reasonableness.

"Whenever possible, for instance, your landlord must give you advance notice of any intrusion into your quarters and must arrive only during normal business hours.

"Florida tenants, incidentally, are protected by special apartment access laws against unauthorized

intrusions by a landlord or landlord employees.

"Such laws specify the limited set of circumstances under which a landlord may enter your apartment...

"Your landlord may not arrive at your door at whim to chat or to snoop on you and your guests.

"Whenever your landlord has no legitimate purpose for entry, you may reasonably refuse admittance.

"Additionally, your landlord must warn you beforehand that an intrusion is coming, assuming the visit is reasonably timed as well.

"The landlord's limited entry rights cannot be abused. Laws prohibit the landlord from using entry privileges to harass tenants.

"In this regard, again, UWF dorm housing contracts contain an illegal clause:

"Authorized University Personnel may enter rooms for normal inspection and maintenance purposes. The resident's personal property is not subject to search without express approval of the resident except when a reasonable belief exists that the room is being used for a purpose which is illegal or which would seriously interfere with discipline and/or personal safety."

"The fact is, a busybody landlord cannot enter your apartment or invade your privacy at whim. So the next time your landlord pays you a meddlesome surprise visit and arrives banging at your door, try this procedure:

"•Ask your landlord's purpose.

"•Tell your landlord you are not obliged to give admittance except for legitimate building related purposes.

"•If your landlord offers you a quickly trumped up but **'legitimate'** *excuse for entry, but also imposes on you in a way that's legally unreasonable, tell the land-*

lord to leave and return another day.

"•Your landlord must give you advance notification of arrival and must time any visit at a reasonable hour.

"•If your landlord persists with demands of admittance, remind the landlord that the law gives you the exclusive right to possession. That right is superior to any outsider's—including the landlord's.

"•Suggest a more convenient time for you to allow the landlord admittance to your premises.

"•If the landlord continues to randomly appear at your door under unreasonable circumstances, sue for money damages for the annoyance caused you.

"Specifically, hit the landlord with the legal citation for the Florida apartment access law.

"Just remember: it's actual trespassing for your landlord to barge in on you unannounced or without advance notification.

*"Each time you let your landlord break your **covenant of quiet enjoyment**, you not only forfeit your own tenant rights, but you also make it harder for other tenants living in your complex to uphold theirs."*

Monday, 26 October 1981

§

Ways to prevent illegal tenant lockout

*"UWF's housing office is penalizing dorm residents who make partial but late room rent payments with an illegal practice known in legal circles as an **'oppressive self–help measure.'***

*"Any campus resident who has even a partial **'past due'** housing account balance now receives an illegal*

*eviction notice requiring the student to **'move out of campus housing within 48 hours and officially surrender the room for the balance of the semester.'***

*"Contrary to this new 'oppressive' policy, UWF housing director **Bill Hudnall** last February told this writer in a published **Voyager** interview that **'we are not going to evict students on the basis of late rent.'***

"No mention of this new eviction policy is made in the latest 1981–82 UWF student housing contracts.

*"At its worst extreme, this eviction action becomes something called **'distress and distraint,'** meaning the tenant is locked out, while the tenant's goods are locked in.*

"But in most jurisdictions, landlords cannot legally lock tenants out of their living units without a court order.

"Most states, including Florida, require landlords to use the statutory eviction process, which guarantees the tenant both notice and a court hearing.

*"When a tenant lockout occurs, the landlord usually denies the tenant both occupancy of the living unit(**distress**)and access to personal possessions left in the residence(**distraint**)—primitive ways to satisfy a landlord's claim for unpaid rent dating back to feudal times.*

"If tenants seriously want to end such outmoded and 'oppressive self–help measures,' they must become informed and willing to fight for their legal tenant rights.

"Here's what to do when facing an illegal lockout:

"•Phone the police and complain of an illegal trespass. A landlord has no more right than a stranger to enter your home, seize and lock your personal prop-

208

erty; an illegal lockout breaches your right to '**quiet enjoyment**' of your premises and wrongfully takes your property(**conversion**).

"In short, an illegal lockout is the equivalent of trespassing in your home—and can be punishable with criminal penalties.

"•An aggressive lawyer can easily get you a court order returning you to your home on quick notice.

"•If you can't get free legal aid, the court and attorney fee costs and other damages suffered(like motel, food and transportation bills)can often be recovered from offending landlords in a civil damage action.

"•Where the landlord does not physically possess the living unit, local laws in some jurisdictions allow you to simply re–enter your premises.

"CAUTION: police will likely refuse to help you—even though they're authorized to do so—and refer to civil court for a legal remedy to your individual lockout problem…"

Monday, 2 November 1981

§

PJC–UWF unification leads to backdoor sellout of PJC

"Florida citizens and their legislators may soon realize that the best way to preserve our state community college system from threatened destruction is by a merger of Florida State University with the University of West Florida in Pensacola.

"At stake are the educational benefits of open access and equal opportunity given by community colleges to all Florida residents statewide.

"The Pensacola Junior College and UWF presidents last January together proposed merging their different schools under a vague 'unification' plan so that each school could supposedly keep its separate identity.

"Inconsistent and contradictory public statements by former opponents–turned–backers of the PJC–UWF merger showed that a better euphemism than 'union' for the proposal would be the backdoor sellout of PJC.

"'The mission of a college is much different from a university. I fail to see how either school would benefit if they merge,' **State Rep. Tom Patterson** told PJC's **Corsair** student newspaper.

"Said UWF President **James Robinson** in June 1980 during a Pensacola interview with **WEAR–TV** broadcaster **Taris Savell**: 'It's(the merger)unrealistic. Junior colleges, sometimes called community colleges, have objectives and functions to perform that are different from those of universities. The universities are more statewide in their orientation. It is unbecoming of the University of West Florida to try to alter PJC's mission.'

"In July 1980, Robinson told UWF's **Voyager** student newspaper he 'vigorously opposed' any kind of PJC–UWF merger, saying that UWF 'has every reason to respect PJC because the mission of PJC is important and different than the mission of UWF.'

"The Escambia County Commission many months ago likewise voted in a Pensacola resolution to **oppose** merging UWF with **any** other college–level school— PJC included.

"At the time, both PJC and UWF presidents eagerly endorsed the commission vote, both agreeing that a merger of their schools would **not** best serve the inter-

ests of their county.

"Understandably, the PJC–UWF faculties and support personnel, worried mainly about keeping their jobs, generally accept the merger scheme since their presidents have each promised to maintain regular staff levels and retain current academic curriculums.

"So the PJC–UWF merger design has something for both sides: with it, PJC tries to stop UWF's failed four–year expansion effort, while UWF wants to prevent its own merger with FSU.

"But some plain and simple facts show how UWF—despite contrary but false denials by special interest groups—would inevitably and totally 'absorb' PJC under any so–called 'uniting' concept.

*"First, UWF's **President Robinson** at a recent **UWF Foundation Board of Directors** meeting re–affirmed his goal of creating at UWF a lower division of freshman and sophomores as part of a plan to 'stabilize' UWF's stagnant enrollment figures and financial support—which is based on enrollment.*

*"Second, the **Long Range Planning Task Force** of the **Pensacola Area Chamber of Commerce**, of which **Tom Patterson** is a member, likewise re–confirmed its commitment to a four–year UWF by September 1985.*

"Third, special interest groups pushing a PJC–UWF merger now want to gain the greatest possible amount of local and regional consensus on the issue before losing any political supporters with the completion of re–apportionment.

"The Pensacola business sector strongly favors a four–year UWF, obviously, since a bigger prestige image for the university fits in with an overall statewide strategy to use universities as cheap labor pools for outside industries Florida wants to attract.

"Of course, many West Floridians feared losing out to more populated and urbanized areas for the state-wide representation and influence after the once–a–decade re–drawing of legislative districts, using the latest U.S. Census figures, was done in 1982.

"So any PJC–UWF merger idea is nothing but a thinly disguised, backdoor attempt by special interests to get for UWF the four–year status it failed to wrest from the 1981 Florida legislature.

"As State Sen. Tom Tobiassen put it, the only difference between a PJC–UWF merger or union 'is that one begins with a 'U' and the other begins with an 'M.'

"Believing that UWF's expansion is inevitable and unstoppable, well–meaning PJC officials are playing politics with PJC's future in a good–intentioned but short–sighted struggle to save college programs and employee positions.

"Even if any PJC–UWF merger allowed each school to keep its present identity and philosophy, as the planners claim, then the undertaking would surely harm what has been called open educational **'access'** *in at least two ways:*

"First, tuition costs would be higher. Since university tuition is about $10 per credit hour more than junior college tuition, full–time PJC students may each pay up to $150 per semester more to attend a merger school.

"Second, stricter **upper level** *entrance requirements would hurt access. While PJC might keep its 'open door' policy of offering academic and vocational training to anyone having a Florida high school diploma, UWF would continue its more selective policy of forming an elite and exclusive student body.*

"As a result, junior college students who successfully finish two years of lower division academic work

would no longer be able to **automatically** *continue their remaining upper level studies—unless they first passed the one–shot, high–pressure situation of some academically invalid and irrelevant admissions test.*

"In other words, a two–year associate degree or its academic equal would not necessarily guarantee students their rightful opportunity to higher education in Florida.

"As usual, the low–income and minority students who lack either the financial means or mobility to seek education elsewhere would suffer most by the self–serving aims of those having an indifferent and callous disregard for the plight of disadvantaged families.

"Future parts of this series will discuss how contaminating the public services of community colleges with the student–abusive policies and practices of a school like UWF would mean irreversible tragedy for PJC and the entire community college system.

"More importantly, the preferred choice of an FSU–UWF merger for Pensacola over a PJC–UWF merger will be examined in greater detail."

Tuesday, 6 July 1982

§

UWF needs full–time professional counselors, reader says

"One view of public service holds that public authorities exist to serve, not rule their customer public.

"Public offices—including those administering our state universities—likewise exist to service, not subjugate their paying customers.

213

"In turn, official public servants should as far as possible, satisfy the needs and wants of their patrons.

"So public policies and procedures should, as much as possible, naturally bias and weight themselves in favor of, instead of against, the public served.

"And university officials and faculty should treat students as adults and not subjects since, after all, students are consumers who earn and pay for the education they get.

"At the University of West Florida in Pensacola, official help–minded aid for students of any kind is commonly scarce.

"Official hindrance for students at UWF is the rule—not the exception.

"Tragically, most UWF students passively and without resistance submit to the many school injustices they endure.

"For whatever reasons, most UWF students fail to object to the school abuses they suffer with an oddly mute tolerance.

"The bottom line is:

"Because UWF faculty and administrators are probably more student–oppressive and unresponsive than those at any other state university, merging Florida State University with UWF may be the only way left to save Florida's entire community college system from sure ruin.

"To see precisely how the student–abusive policies of UWF would spoil the public services of Pensacola Junior College and endanger the preferred workings of our community colleges, just compare how each school treats its students.

"Academic Advising: UWF Arts and Sciences Dean Lucius F. Ellsworth brags that UWF's school catalog or bulletin 'is not a contract' but excitedly backs its

dictum that, 'The counselor has the authority to plan a program for a student in excess of the minimums listed.'

*"In other words, an academic counselor at UWF can pick for students **extra** courses to take—over and above the 'minimums' specified as **necessary** for graduation by either particular academic departments or general university degree regulations.*

"If a UWF student rightly refuses to be forced by a counselor to waste personal time, effort, and money in taking such extra and unwanted classes, a petty or spiteful counselor can cancel all degree planning and disqualify the student from graduation.

"The counselors holding these excessive powers of discretion over student degree planning at UWF are but mere faculty members assigned to students without choice within and by particular academic departments.

"In practical effect, these so–called UWF counselors can delay a student's graduation indefinitely and at whim—despite the financial hardship or emotional anxiety caused the student in the process.

"UWF economics instructor Janet S Miller has said that when a student chooses to bypass academic advisors during class–scheduling, 'a farce' is made of the counseling process—hard doing since the system was farcical at its invention.

*"Academic advising should be a **voluntary**, not a compulsory process—as it is at Pensacola Junior College—where **professional** full–time counselors are freely available to students readily wanting their help.*

*"But academic counseling amounts to academic coercion at UWF, where academic intimidators called counselors are **imposed** on students who are often un-*

willing to enroll for the unrequired courses dictated to them.

"What's worse, most UWF counselors delude themselves into believing that doctoral degrees qualify them to give students 'paternalistic' and unsolicited advice on everything from students' private plans to personal problems.

"But it is highly unlikely that any student attends UWF or any other state university seeking surrogate parents.

"That's why obligatory academic advising should be outlawed outright—and why Florida must not allow UWF to damage with its shortcomings and failures the better ways of our community colleges."

Monday, 12 July 1982

§

"Joe—I agree with you whole–heartedly. **F Biasco**, *7/15/82*
"We need to treat our students as adults—indeed they are—and not as children." **FB**

§

Students must speak up to learn in educational environment

"Today's so–called 'Me Generation' of college and university students seem to be a tame, even servile lot—committed to little else but themselves, if anything—but for reasons different from what you might think. And even that could be an understatement.

"Comatose, in fact, might be a better word to describe them with. Seldom now, after all, do students

stage marches, rallies, sit–ins, class–boycotts or cam-
pus building take–overs to protest social injustice,
much less advocate social change.

*"**Livingston College** student dean **Michele**
LeMoal and **Upsala College** student dean **Barbara**
Bender in a recent study reported that student dem-*
onstrations on college campuses nationwide have
fallen 11 percent since the Free Speech Movement at
Berkeley kicked off the turbulent student protest move-
ments of the 1960s.

"Between the fall of 1978 and the winter of 1980 the
educators randomly surveyed 205 schools of higher
learning and found that, during that period, dem-
onstrations happened on 46 percent of the campuses,
compared to 57 percent reported in like surveys done
in the middle and late 1960s.

"But that doesn't mean that students no longer care
about social issues and causes—clearly they do. In
the late 1970s, students demonstrated strongly over
black students' rights, nuclear power, financial aid
cutbacks, faculty tenure, and U.S. meddling in El
Salvador, the report said.

"Yet only 11 percent of the demonstrations actually
disrupted college activity, the study added. Subjects
of those demonstrations took in Iran, nuclear power,
tenure, homosexual and Hispanic students' rights.

"Nowadays, tragically, most students are little
more than college faculty puppets or administrative
playthings.

"And when you think about it, it's really a crisis
situation:

"Students literally run circles through the bureau-
cratic maze of their favorite 'diploma mill,' bowing
to every rule, regulation, and procedure—all with-
out question, let alone objection—and no matter how

much the rules offend or hurt them.

"Then they jump at the constant beck and call of any professor or administrator who might summon them to do their whimsical bidding. And even if they do manage to muster the boldness and daring to disagree and argue with their 'superiors,' before it's over they'll usually let themselves be bullied and browbeaten into willing submission.

"After all, when school officials command, students obey—without question, without resistance. And when school command notices and decrees come to their mailboxes, they submit quietly and comply—also without challenge or opposition.

"Speak for yourself, you might naturally be thinking. Or you might feel that most school policies and practices are really not that bad, nor are they really worth fighting against anyhow.

"Either way, if you're a student, you've most likely taken the system–imposed role of being among all the other docile learners who know their place, keep quiet, and simply do what they're told.

"So the reason that students are supposedly so apathetic and uninvolved—far from being indifferent to the great social questions of their time—is that they've just let themselves be fooled into being obedient servants of their school rulers."

Monday, 25 October 1982

§

"Dear Joe–

*"Glad you liked the St. Bernard photo that Jim Rhine put in The **Voyager**. No one else did. We were ready to kill him since another picture should have gone in*

that space.

*"Anyway, I am writing to tell you that my time as editor has come to an end. The managing editor, Joy Davies, will be taking my place as I finish my last semester at The **Pensacola News** as an intern.*

"Thanks for the controversial copy the last few months. In one way or another we've enjoyed it.

"Chris."—Chris & Paul McLester, Christmas card, 23 December 1982

§

Ironically, the truest poetic just deserts was actually getting *paid* by the *Voyager* student newspaper their standard journalistic remuneration for writing all those printed anti–UWF establishment *"special contributions"*—as the editors labeled them!

Now I'll make even more money by publicly exposing with this book the crimes of UWF's most invidious knaves and villains.

Ah, *justice* is truly **SWEET!**

But the truest *best* justice by far is finally exposing to full public view the outright rampant bigotry of the UWF Establishment!

"Chancellor Newell has asked me to respond to your letter of June 16, 1982, in which you allege various improprieties by the administration at the University of West Florida," **Steve McArthur**, indifferent do–nothing and good–for–nothing Vice Chancellor, Administration & Support, for the State University System of Florida wrote me in his excruciatingly curt and pompous letter dated 28 June 1982. *"It is the opinion of this office that this matter has been adequately investigated and no further action is necessary."*

Nothing was ever "investigated" at all conscientiously much less "adequately."

Now let the court of public opinion judge and decide what "further action" could and should be "necessary."

PART III:

POETIC

JUST

DESERTS

(WHAT GOES AROUND COMES AROUND INDEED!)

This section shall be regularly revised and updated to report how the most poetic just deserts of that inevitable(and inescapable) *Judgment Day* finally catches up to condemn all the evil–minded UWF knaves and villains who—as recounted faithfully in this book—most maliciously abused and mis–used their imperious positions of official bureaucratic authority to deliberately and purposely coerce, intimidate, oppress, persecute, repress, threaten or otherwise aggrieve, victimize and trample upon the rights of blameless students they were supposed to humbly serve rather than subjugate.

This is done to demonstrate the powerfully profound but simple heartening fact of life that—with time and universal justice—the wicked *black* justice so wrongly committed and perpetrated by even the most rancorous, spiteful, treacherous, vicious and unscrupulous of depraved degenerates can *never prevail forever!*

That twirp UWF collections manager, *Phillip M Waltrip*—as a prime sample—actually got elected to be a short–lived district 2 Escambia County commissioner in the early 1980s. According to the county's "campaign treasurer's report" several of UWF's most familiar knaves and villains actually contributed to twirp Waltrip's campaign coffers:
  ·*E.W. Hopkins*: $200(9/17/83)
  ·*Lucius Ellsworth*: $50(10/17/83)
Around the same period UWF propagandist, *Jerry L Maygarden,* got elected to be a short–lived district 2 Pensacola city councilman whose campaign coffers likewise got contributed to by familiar UWF knaves and villains:
  ·*E.W. Hopkins*: $200(3/22/85)
  ·*Lucius F. Ellsworth*: $100(3/30/85)

·*F.E. Ranelli*: $50(4/15/85)

Which just goes to prove the old adage: bastards who lie together stick together!

UWF students can jubilantly celebrate and gleefully take heart though that most if not all of those bastards from UWF's corrupt good old boy network are no longer around to victimize them—and not a moment too soon! Doubtless they'll *all* learn sooner or later, one way or other, that *none* of them are immune to the grievous adversity or hardship they so coldly and callously inflicted on others. Here's the run–down to date about how either justice or mortality or both brought them all to pay the piper and settle *their* accounts—*in full*:

·CR Bennett, **DEAD**(79), 19 February 2019
·Marnette Cook Byrkit,
·Phillip R Campbell, **DEAD**(81), 7 Oct 2002
·Thomas Carrol Committe, **DEAD**(89), 16 Jul 2012
·Charles E Clark, **DEAD**(74), 17 November 2015
·Kenneth Leroi Curtis, **DEAD**(1 May 2023)
·Arthur H Doerr, **DEAD**(86), 16 June 2011
·Linda Ophelia Dye(retired, 2003)
·Richard Charles Einbecker(retired, 1991)
·Clarence Couch Elebash, **DEAD**(96), 16 April 2022
·Lucius Fuller Ellsworth,
·Thomas Watts Henderson,
·Elbert Wesley Hopkins, **DEAD**(97), 28 October 2025
·Bill M Hudnall,
·Huey L Latham. **DEAD**(92), 14 July 2024
·Jerry Louis Maygarden,
·James I Miklovich, **DEAD**(78), 17 August 2020
·Janet Claire Stormont Miller, **DEAD**(80), 16

November 2021
- Frank Edward Ranelli,
- James A Robinson, **DEAD**(85), 7 May 2018
- Phillip Malcolm Waltrip,

PART IV:
EPILOGUE

"We are deeply saddened by this horrific tragedy. At this time, we find little meaning in these senseless acts. We know we can come together as the law school family in a loving, caring, supportive way. Each of us is suffering, but as a family, we can find strength to pass through this terrible dark and tragic valley."— **Lucius F Ellsworth, president, Appalachian School of Law, news conference, 16 January 2002**

Peter Odighizuwa, a 43–year–old Nigerian law student and naturalized U.S. citizen rampaged in early 2002 at the *Appalachian School of Law*, shooting and killing in their offices dean *L. Anthony Sutin*, 42, and associate professor *Thomas Blackwell*, 41, resorting to a Jennings .380–calibre semiautomatic pistol to commit the crimes.

Peter, a former teacher from Dayton, Ohio, had been brusquely dismissed for reportedly bad grades and his financial aid summarily suspended.

Naturally, when somebody is driven to embark on a murderous rampage they're automatically and witlessly branded as being "disgruntled," a "loner," "paranoid" or "sick."

Hell, I'm a so–called "loner" myself—and proud of it!—but I wouldn't stupidly sacrifice my personal freedom to blow away blustering bureaucratic functionaries who aren't even worth the cost of the bullets!

But you have to be *driven*—out of profound frustration and despair that turns to supreme desperation—to go to such drastic and extreme lengths to redress a real and valid grievance.

And I *know* smug and smirking "Provost," *Lucius F Ellsworth*—as I *personally experienced* how brazenly arrogant he actually is when, with his flabby jowls wobbling, he haughtily condescended to tell me in his high and mighty manner that the UWF catalog wasn't a "contract" and that some equally dorky "counselor"(*Janet S Miller*)could get off scot–free, dictating in her own cocky manner that I'd be forced to unwillingly waste time, effort and money taking a useless elective "money and banking" course required for graduation by neither the UWF economics department nor the university at large.

And I'm quite confident, having absolutely no doubt whatever that Ellsworth stamped his characteristically insolent tone on the administration of the *Appalachian School of Law* during his tenure as president there.

So it's scarcely surprising to me that such a not–so–"senseless" act could be provoked under any college or university administration presided over by such an imperious and high–handed bureaucratic functionary as Ellsworth.

That's why such a tragic incident serves as both a cautionary warning and lesson to bossy bureaucrats everywhere: take care whom you so outrageously offend and do wrongful injury and injustice to—or you could very well suffer the deadly consequences for your callous and contemptuous disregard for common courtesy and human decency.

"It's so heartwarming to see this," Ellsworth reportedly blustered after the tragic incident. *"There's no doubt that out of this tragedy, this community has united...As horrific as this has been, I'm certain the institution will be stronger."*

Even after three people perished under the coercive and oppressive administration he doubtless fostered and promoted so painstakingly, Ellsworth just still doesn't get it—that he's responsible and answerable for the consequences of his shameless, brazen–faced arrogance.

§

Buffoonish Blockhead*(CR)Bennett*—ever the stupidly second–guessing bureaucratic functionary like the rest of his cohorts comprising UWF's corrupt good old boy network—once presumptuously chastised me, not knowing me from Adam, for not returning to *Florida Atlantic University(FAU)*in Boca Raton to finish my attempted master's degree in political science—for which I completed all graduate course work shy a comprehensive examination and master's thesis. The simple fact was: I'd already deliberately discarded any idea of ever finishing that master's degree at *FAU*—another story altogether.

Though seemingly less ambitious I had—unbeknownst to Blockhead Bennett or any of his corrupt cohorts—a much simpler but far more forthright and straightforward agenda in mind:

•live cheaply on–campus at UWF to remain in my backwater hometown of Pensacola to be near my fresh Chinese girlfriend and at the same time seduce multiple campus co–eds the length and breadth of the land—as more graphically recounted in my book, *Sexcapades by the Decades: The Twenties*.

•pick up the worthless second *bachelor's of economics degree* from worthless UWF wrongfully denied me in 1976.

•pick up at *Pensacola Junior College(PJC)*the single course left titled, *"Police Operations"(CCJ1420)*, required for me to complete in June 1980 the *associate of science(AS)*degree in *law enforcement*, which I'd left unfinished in 1974.

•pick up likewise at *PJC* in December 1981 the state–commissioned *police recruit academy training certificate(CCJ0101)*, which was the natural adjunct to the AS law enforcement degree.

•pick up by October 1981 as a matter of strictly incidental convenience yet a *third* worthless *bachelor's degree* from worthless UWF in *international studies*—especially since its four so–called *"core courses"* comprised *next to nil* in the way of "graduation requirements."

Throughout that time of tying up all those loose academic ends, my primary aspiration was to muck-rake and raise a mighty ruckus over UWF's corrupt bureaucratic officials and their imperious *policies and practices!*

MISSION ACCOMPLISHED IN ALL RESPECTS!—despite the impotent attempts by UWF's corrupt good old boy network to deliberately impede my endeavors every last step of the way!

As for Alice, she became a US citizen with my aid and flowered and thrived like the tender bloom she was, excelling at her first love of art at San Francisco's prestigious *Academy of Art College*.

Receiving a letter like this though made the entire experience perfectly worthwhile:

§

"Dear Mr. Covino:

"I am writing to congratulate you on your article that appeared in the **Voyager** *entitled 'UWF needs full–time professional counselors.' I whole–heartedly agree with your assertion that UWF's faculty and adminis-trators are student–oppressive and that a merger with* **Florida State University** *may be the only way to save 'Florida's entire community from sure ruin.'*

"I am a black female and have been subjected not only to UWF's student–oppressive policies, but its racially oppressive one as well. But, like you, I managed to endure.

"Lastly, your writings have long reflected my view, but I never took the time to write, until now of course.

"If there is anything that I can do to assist you in your effort to promote social justice, do not hesitate to write.

*"Keep up the good work."—**Ms. Gloria J. McCullough,***

JOSEPH COVINO JR

19 July 1982

§

OPPRESSIVE POLICIES AND PRACTICES EXPLOITED BY IMPERIOUS BUREAUCRATIC FUNCTIONARIES TO SUBJUGATE RATHER THAN SERVICE STUDENTS IS ULTIMATELY THE MAIN REASON WHY THIS TIMELESS CAUTIONARY TALE FROM TIMES PAST IS RELEVANT AND VITAL TO CONTEMPORARY STUDENTS OF ANY AGE!

§

At its present website UWF's ***"development"***(pan-handling–and–sponging)office crows that *"private gifts from alumni, friends, employees, businesses and foundations play a vital role in supporting the **mission and vision** of the University of West Florida,"* whining that *"gifts to the University of West Florida are critical to its success. Tuition pays for less than 25 percent of the cost of a UWF education, and state support alone is not enough to deliver high quality programs that meet the needs of our state and region,"* mis–representing itself with pure puffery that *"your gift to any area of campus you choose could: help a first generation college student be the first in his family to graduate college..."*

Amongst its core ***"values"*** UWF claims quite speciously that of ***"Integrity:*** *doing the right things for the right reasons,"* and amongst its so–called ***"standards of excellence:*** *courtesy, flexibility and responsiveness."*

Well, in the late 1970s and early 1980s I got a caus-

233

tic taste of that abysmal lower–learning institution's spurious practice of courtesy, flexibility and responsiveness: even today UWF can cry the poor–mouth for charitable contributions, and yet countenance in good conscience an arrogant "counselor" callously calling an underprivileged student—the "first in his family to graduate college"—a "sob story" whilst high–handedly inflicting the added hardship of an elective but illegitimate "graduation requirement."

Once when I explained my strapped predicament to smug and smirking student affairs director, **Linda O Dye**, she hurriedly fumbled in her desk to hand over to me some free–ride tokens for the city bus that didn't even come to campus!

And just *what* exactly is this abysmal lower–learning institution's so–called "***mission and vision***?" To ruthlessly quash the most innocuous form of democratic dissent—the exercise of First Amendment free speech and expression in critical journalistic articles, opinion columns and public speeches?

And just *how* exactly does this abysmal lower–learning institution preserve its so–called "*integrity*" in doing all the **right** things for all the **right** reasons? By exploiting the oppressive policies and practices of its various bureaucratic offices as devious devices to inflict administrative punishment on student "undesirables?"

UWF is in essence a corrupt establishment run by evil–minded, malicious and vicious bureaucratic functionaries.

With this book then I appeal in closing to all potential UWF donors and benefactors: give or donate nothing to UWF as it gives no charity and so merits none in return.

To all prospective students I appeal to conscien-

234

tiously and vociferously object, protest and raise in defiant dissent your most demanding voice against the ruthless tyranny of imperious bureaucratic dictatorships and their official dictators!

Proper questions must be asked
by
Dr. Erskine S. Dottin

(reprinted from his *"View From The Campus"* opinion column published in the *Pensacola News–Journal*)

"Someone once said that 'the mark of an educated person is not his/her ability to answer questions, but his/her ability to raise proper questions.' The literature these days is filled with educated persons providing answers to the problems in American education. Very few educational reformers seem interested in raising proper questions.

"However, I came across someone who seemed to raise proper questions about the educational establishment, especially and more specifically the public high school.

"I found the questions raised by the writer vital for students of education. The questions seemed particularly germane to educational policymakers, especially those in power positions in government.

"The writer asked a simple, yet provocative question, 'What is the function of the public high school in American society?' He then went on to raise some proper questions:

"Is it to educate in the sense of reinforcing community values, of training students to accept the norms of their social environment? Or to educate in the sense of teaching them to discover their minds, to think for themselves, to pursue the truth wherever it leads? In doing the one, is the other undone?

"Can the school teach students to think for themselves and not cause them to question traditional norms? Or should students even question such things? Or should they question them as long as they accept them in the end? Or is it even important to question, since life must be lived in any case? Or should students be shielded from questions? Or does it depend on the students? On his/her age? On his/her maturity? Or are there things students should never question? Or should they be taught not to question but just to accept? Is it healthy or unhealthy to question? Or is it healthy to question, but not too much?

"Are students' minds owned by their parents? Do parents have the right to bring their children up in their own ideas? Is this the instilling of proper values or brainwashing? Ought parents to expect that the school will teach what they think is right? That it will not contradict what is taught in the home?

"Can students be victimized by any of this? Or do they have the right to be educated in the way they want? Or are they too young and inexperienced to know? Must they be guided? Can they be guided and at the same time warped? Do intelligent students have the right to the kind of an education of which their less gifted parents might not approve? Do intelligent parents have the right to have their less gifted children educated in a way which may be beyond their capacity or interests?

"Does the community which pays the school bills have a legitimate say in any of this? Does it have the right to determine what the school teaches, to ensure that only its own values are taught? Or does the community delegate its authority to the school and trust the school's judgment to teach what it thinks best for students.

"Should the school teach community values? Is education into community values proper upbringing or propaganda? Is what one agrees with truth and disagrees with propaganda? Or are there many truths? Or none? Or is it all relative? Or is there only one truth? As determined by whom? For everyone.

"And if the school should teach community values, then the values of which segment of the community? The conservatives? The liberals? The moderates? All of them? Or just the majority? Or the minority? Or the most vocal? Or should national values be taught. Who determines what they are? Should the values of other countries and cultures be taught? As being better than community or national values? As being worse? Or the same? Is an education which affirms community and national values ethnocentrism? Or the proper formation of the young? Should the community control the school? Or is this thought–control? Or are some forms of thought–control permissible?

"Or should the school even teach values? Or should it teach only facts? Or by not teaching values, does it reinforce community values by remaining silent about others? Or does the school have the right or responsibility to expose students to values and viewpoints of which they may have never heard? To take them out of their place and time? To have them see their community and nation through other eyes and as simply part of a wide world? Should the school criticize these other viewpoints if different from the community's? Or should it simply present and explain them as different? As wrong? Or as equally valid?

"What is the teacher's role in all of this? To teach what the community wants? Or what they may feel is best for students? Should teachers be controlled by the community which pays their salaries? Can they in conscience teach what the community wants if they disagree with it? Or should they teach what the community wants as only one view among many? Should they teach all points of view as possible, and have the students decide for themselves? Or do students need the security of only one point of view? Or just some students?

"Should tolerance for all ideas be taught in school? Or only for those with which the community already agrees? Is open–mindedness good for students? But not too much? Would it only confuse them? Is open–mindedness a form of indoctrination? Or lack of conviction? Or is lack conviction open–mindedness? Is closed–mindedness the courage of keeping to one's convictions a form of closed–mindedness?

"Do children exist for the community or the community for its children? To whom does the school owe responsibility? The community or its students? Or both? Are their interests the same? Are students' interests served if they are taught to accept community values or to think for themselves?

"Or only if they are taught to do both? Or is this contradictory?

"What should the school serve? The past or the future?

"What solution do you have to the foregoing questions? As a parent? As a community member? As a community leader? As a student? As a child? As the president of the local university? As the local superintendent of schools? As a member of the local political delegation to Tallahasse? As an educated person?"

www.ingramcontent.com/pod-product-compliance
Lightning Source LLC
Chambersburg PA
CBHW021224090426

42740CB00006B/375